Answer Your Call

*Reclaim God's Purpose for
Faith, Family, and Work*

DICK AND MARTHA LYLES

SERVANT
BOOKS

PUBLISHED BY FRANCISCAN MEDIA
Cincinnati, Ohio

LIBRARY OF CONGRESS CATALOGING-IN-PUBLICATION DATA
Lyles, Richard I.
Answer your call : reclaim God's purpose for faith, family, and work / Dick and Martha Lyles.
pages cm
Includes bibliographical references and index.
ISBN 978-1-61636-540-0 (alk. paper)
1. Christian life—Catholic authors. I. Lyles, Martha. II. Title.
BX2350.3.L95 2013
248.4'82—dc23
2012046104
ISBN 978-1-61636-540-0

Published by Servant Books, an imprint of Franciscan Media
28 W. Liberty St.
Cincinnati, OH 45202
www.FranciscanMedia.org

Printed in the United States of America.
Printed on acid-free paper.
13 14 15 16 17 5 4 3 2 1

CONTENTS

*We dedicate this book to
Charlotte, Sophie, Luke, Lyla, Lucy, Emma, and Levi—
our adorable and adoring grandchildren.
We fervently hope that someday these words
will help you and many others in your generation
to hear and answer God's call for you.*

ACKNOWLEDGMENTS

First, we owe a debt of gratitude to our beloved assistant, Marsha Wilson, who helped us through many drafts before we finally created one good enough to bring forth for publication. She was and will always be a shining light in our lives, even though she was called home before the book was finally published.

Thanks also to Claudia Volkman, our editor at Servant, for sharing our vision and passion for the project and for all her tremendous effort in clearing up our attributions and references. Thanks also to the entire team at Servant for their creativity in marketing, the wonderful cover design, and all the things necessary to bring a project like this to successful fruition.

We owe special thanks to Matt Manion, the CEO of the Catholic Leadership Institute in Pennsylvania for the many insights, anecdotes, quotes, and ideas he contributed to the book. Matt, you are a shining example both of enlightened leadership and of someone who has truly discerned his call and is answering that call to the fullest. The impact The Catholic Leadership Institute is having on the Church and on Catholics throughout North America will be felt in a powerfully positive manner for generations to come.

We also owe special thanks to our dear friend and colleague Christina Capecchi, who helped polish the manuscript and also provided many quotes and anecdotes. She is a phenomenal writer and "human support system," to whom we are immensely grateful.

Also deserving of our appreciation is Karen Walker, CEO of *The Catholic Business Journal* (catholicbusinessjournal.biz) who has helped move this project forward every step of the way. *The Catholic Business Journal* also sponsors *The Catholic Business Hour with Dick Lyles,* broadcast live every Saturday morning on EWTN's global radio network. This book would not be as rich as it is nor have as many examples, if it were not for the many conversations Dick has conducted with callers during the past several years.

And finally, thank you, Archbishop Naumann, for writing the foreword and for your support for our efforts.

A president from one of our Catholic high schools shared an e-mail he had received from one of the school's recent graduates. She was completing her first year of college at a large state university. She asked the president to thank all of the faculty and staff of the high school for preparing her so well for college.

However, she was even more grateful for the formation she had received in the Catholic Faith. She was pleased to discover that she had the internal strength to remain true to her convictions in an environment not supportive of and even at times openly hostile to her Catholic Faith.

She also shared that she was in a sorority where many of her sorority sisters did not share her beliefs and moral values. However, she said that they respected her and asked her many questions about her faith. This young woman was convinced she was at this secular university in part to help her sorority sisters get to heaven.

When I first heard Dick Lyles on Catholic radio, I was delighted to discover a program designed to help listeners figure out how they can better live their Catholic Faith in the workplace. This is a central component to what Blessed John Paul II and Pope Benedict XVI labeled "the New Evangelization." It is in the boardrooms and classrooms, laboratories and courthouses, movie studios and office cubicles, sorority houses and student unions that the Catholics are called to transform the culture.

So naturally, when recently I met Dick and his wife, Martha, I was enthused to learn that they had just authored *Answer Your Call*—an immensely practical book to help Catholics discern how to serve God with the unique set of talents and gifts Our Lord has entrusted to them. I found illuminating Dick and Martha's method for integrating faith, family, and service to others in discovering one's unique purpose in life.

The Lyleses' approach is refreshing first of all, because it places faith squarely at the center of the discernment process. Sadly, many Catholics have been swept along by the prevailing cultural winds that exalt personal fulfillment as the ultimate goal in determining life's purpose.

The central question for a Catholic is not: "What do I want to do with my life?" It is not: "How can I make the most money or gain the most fame?" The key question for every Catholic is "What does God want me to do with my life? What is God's plan or dream for me?"

Answer Your Call provides helpful tools for the reader to assess their special gifts and determine where they experience the greatest joy and peace in their utilization. It is only natural when we are using our God-given talents to fulfill the ultimate purpose for which we were created— namely to know, love, and serve God—that we will experience the "abundant life" Jesus promised his disciples.

As a bishop, I spend a significant amount of time promoting priestly vocations. The Church today, as in every age, needs holy and zealous priests. In our society, there are many obstacles to a young man being able to hear and embrace a call to serve the Church as a priest. In such a milieu, it is important for the Church to be very intentional and vigorous in the promotion of vocations to the priesthood.

However, sometimes because of the enthusiastic promotion of priestly vocations, some begin to think that the only "religious vocations" are to the priesthood and the consecrated life. Vatican II emphasized the universal call to holiness. Every baptized Christian is called to live a heroic life of love and service. Priestly vocations are important because priests are the human instruments that God uses in providing to all his people the tools and graces needed to realize holiness.

God has a dream for each of us that is so much greater than what on our own we can envision for ourselves. *Answer Your Call* provides readers with a map to help them discover God's plan for them considering their unique gift mix and amidst the actual circumstances of their lives.

Answer Your Call is so much more than how to manual for making the best career choices. It gives readers a method for discerning God's call in a way that gives proper emphasis to faith, family, and work. *Answer Your Call* gives practical guidance on how to experience that complete joy Our Lord desires for each of us in this world. Ultimately, if we answer God's call it opens the path to heaven not only for ourselves, but also provides us with many opportunities to help others discover that same heavenly road.

Archbishop Joseph F. Naumann
Archdiocese of Kansas City in Kansas

Do you know that you *don't* have to care for the poorest of the poor in Calcutta, serve as pope for twenty-five years, or be burned at the stake to become a saint? Nor is it necessary to die fighting lions in the Colosseum of Rome or be martyred in some other grotesque fashion. Not that all the people who lived or died these ways don't deserve to be elevated—they do. Their sainthood should be valued and cherished. But at the same time we honor these wonderful saints for the way they lived and died, it is equally important to realize that we can each achieve sainthood by following a different path—a path unique to each of us, tied to our own unique call and the gifts given to us by God.

We considered writing a book on how to become a saint but decided not to when we discovered that many people were scared by the concept, daunted by the idea of trying to become a saint with all its sterling implications—unwrinkled, unflappable, unattainable. That's because many people don't understand the concept of sainthood.

Saints are people who have been canonized by the Catholic Church. Canonization is simply a means to proclaim that they practiced heroic virtue and lived in fidelity to God's grace. A primary reason for recognizing certain people in this manner is to sustain the hope of believers by proposing the saints as models and intercessors. More simply stated, saints are people who got it right. They answered their call as human beings by combining their God-given gifts with God's grace to achieve a unique purpose for their lives. In essence, they are people who, without a doubt, made it to heaven. If you want to get to heaven, then for all practical purposes, you want to be a saint. The goals are one in the same.

You, too, can achieve sainthood. The best way to become a saint is to live life to the fullest—to have an eternally fulfilling and wildly rewarding life here on earth, doing the things you are most passionate about and doing them in a way that brings satisfaction and true joy to you and those around you, while also bringing glory to God.

Our intent is simple: to provide you a way to identify and live the most fulfilling path possible for the rest of your life, however long that may be. Our underlying belief is that there are no better guideposts from which to live your life than those of Catholic doctrine. It is the backbone of the oldest Christian faith. With our two-thousand-year tradition of living the teachings of Jesus Christ, with the examples of all the saints who have preceded us, and with all the great writings of Catholic theologians throughout the ages, there simply is no better foundation upon which to build the life for which you were created.

Within this massive foundation of Catholic knowledge, we've developed a framework that helps clarify and put into perspective what we consider the nine most important dimensions of Catholic life.

We each have a unique set of natural gifts that comprise three dimensions: skills, aptitude, and motivation. We have available to us God's supernatural grace, which accrues in three forms: sanctifying, sacramental, and special (or charisms). We also each have a unique life purpose, expressed in three avenues: faith, family, and work. When we successfully combine our three dimensions of natural gifts with the various forms of God's grace to achieve our threefold personal call, we can achieve not only joy and fulfillment but—if we do it right—sanctity, too.

As we begin, it is fitting to consider the words of St. Maximilian Kolbe, the Polish friar who volunteered to die in place of a stranger at a Nazi concentration camp. He said:

Every man and woman in this world has been assigned a mission by God. In fact, ever since God created the universe, He arranged the first causes in such a way that the unbroken chain of their effects should create the most favorable conditions and circumstances for each person to fulfill the mission that God has assigned him or her.

Therefore, every person is born with abilities that are proportionate to the mission he or she has been entrusted, and throughout each person's whole life, the environment, circumstances and everything else will contribute to make it easy and possible for him or her to reach that purpose.

In fact, each person's perfection consists in reaching that purpose; and the more thoroughly one's task is carried out, and the more scrupulously one's mission is fulfilled, the greater and holier he or she shall be before the eyes of God.

Besides natural gifts, each person is also accompanied by the grace of God from the cradle to the tomb. God's grace is poured on us in such quantity and quality that our weak human nature strengthens itself by acquiring the supernatural energy we need to face our own mission.[1]

Cardinal John Henry Newman said it similarly: "God has created me to do him some definite service. He has committed some work to me which he has not committed to another.... I am a link in a chain, a bond of connection between persons. He has not created me for naught. I shall do good, I shall do his work."[2]

Our individuality—including the unique mix of gifts God has given each of us—is our promise. Because of God's expectation that we each contribute something different to the world, our promise represents our distinct potential to make that contribution.

When a professional football team drafts a strong young quarterback, we say the player has promise. When a bright and enthusiastic graduate embarks on an exciting career, we say that person has promise. Likewise, when each of us is born, we also have promise as human beings—promise to bring something special to the world in a way that brings honor to God, our Creator and Father.

Our personal promise represents a type of personal covenant with God: "Lord, you gave me these gifts, and now it's up to me to nurture, develop, and use them to their fullest potential to achieve my unique calling."

If only it were that simple.

The fact is, it's not that simple. If it were, we would look around and see a productive and peaceful world of fulfilled people. But that's not what we see. Why? Because there are a number of factors at work that hinder us from fulfilling this covenant, keeping our promise, and achieving our God-given potential. These factors fall into two categories.

The first category contains all the things that either we do or that happen to us that cause us to lose sight of God, or cause us to fail to recognize his presence in our lives. These factors blind us not only to God's presence, but also to his abundant graces. Some of these forces are evil, but many are simply caused by the complexities of the world in which we live. Because all of these forces are inextricably interwoven with the fabric of our society, it is easy to fall victim to them without realizing it. By understanding these blinders we have an opportunity to look beyond them to see the very special miracles and the supernatural grace God makes available to us every day. Chapters one through six address the most common of these blinders.

Only after we understand how these blinders limit our vision can we become empowered to live our lives in a more deliberate, meaningful way. In essence, we will inoculate ourselves against becoming victims to the blinders that denied us this grace in the past.

The second category contains influences that cause people to lose sight of (or never see in the first place) their own natural gifts. Again, many of these influences are merely the result of the dizzyingly complex world in which we live. We need to overcome them in order to see our gifts and blessings clearly so we can bring them to bear on a meaningful life's purpose. These influences are addressed in chapters seven through ten.

This book will take you through a process to discern your God-given purpose in life, understand your own natural gifts, and develop a plan to overcome all those blinders and influences so you can connect more deeply with God's abundant graces on a path that will lead to true fulfillment. Chapters eleven through sixteen explain how to do this. Chapter twelve describes in detail the three areas of your life that will be transformed as you learn to hear and answer your call. The remaining chapters will guide you through a process to help you identify your call in the context of these three areas and help you to develop a simple plan that will lead to the true fulfillment of God's promise to you.

This process takes time. It's not something you can complete in a few hours or even a few days. For some it may take years, as it did with some of our saints. Consider St. Augustine, for example. He didn't even become a Christian until well into adulthood, and he then became one of the greatest Catholic theologians and philosophers. How much time it will take you to find your call and start down your path to fulfillment depends on you. The most important thing you can do now is to make a genuine commitment to God, yourself, and your family that you will work hard to discern every dimension of your call and then live it. We hope you'll decide there's no nobler undertaking—that your most important legacy will be the example you set with your life. And, of course, we hope that this book will in some meaningful way contribute to that effort. *Answer Your*

Call is intentionally concise, written for today's typical Catholic: people who are busy, and who, for a variety of reasons, may not be achieving their potential in their faith, in their relationships, or in their careers. It's also written for young people who have not yet traveled far in their life's journey. We hope they will discover this book early enough that it can help them avoid even a temporary stint of unfulfilling endeavors.

Don't turn to the back of the book first!

Many readers will want to jump to the back of the book and start the "how to" activities first, thinking they can take a shortcut to success. If you do, you'll be taking a shortcut that will turn out to be a detour. The first two sections of the book are important in helping you free yourself from some of the blinders and influences that may have constrained you in the past. If you don't know them and understand them, it's likely you'll carry them forward into your future—something you definitely want to avoid.

—Dick and Martha Lyles

Consult not your fears but your hopes and your dreams. Think not about your frustrations, but about your unfulfilled potential. Concern yourself not with what you tried and failed in, but what is still possible for you to do.[3]

—Pope John XXIII

PART ONE

How We Lose Sight of God's Presence

We achieve sanctity by combining God's supernatural graces with our natural gifts to fulfill the unique purpose God has designed for each of us. One way many of us fall short of reaching our full potential is that we lose sight of God's presence. By losing sight of his presence, we deny ourselves the opportunity of experiencing the fullness of His supernatural graces.

Are any of these blinders causing you to lose sight of God's presence in your life and keeping you from embracing his abundant grace?

CHAPTER ONE

Lack of Recognition

Chapter 24 of the Gospel of Luke begins on Easter Sunday. That same day, two of Jesus's followers were walking toward the village of Emmaus. Suddenly Jesus joined them, but they didn't recognize him. Jesus asks them what they are discussing so intensely. "They stood still, looking sad" (Luke 24:17). Finally one of them said, "Are you the only visitor to Jerusalem who does not know the things that have happened here in these days?" They proceeded to fill Jesus in on all the events leading up to the crucifixion and how they all had hoped Jesus would be he one to redeem Israel. They ended by saying that now Jesus's body is missing from the tomb and how the women who had discovered this had heard from an angel that Jesus was alive.

Jesus walked along with them, interpreting the Scriptures and explaining everything about himself to them. When they reached the village, the two disciples invited Jesus to stay with them, still unaware of who he was. And then

> When he was at table with them, he took the bread and blessed and broke it, and gave it to them. And their eyes were opened and they recognized him; and he vanished out of their sight. (Luke 24:30–31)

How does your perspective compare to that of the Emmaus disciples? What if we limit the comparison to your *work* life? Far too often we recognize God's grace and his presence at church or when we receive the sacraments while ignoring—or at least failing to recognize—his presence, and especially his grace, in our work- , business- , or career-related activities.

In spite of the reality (as stated by St. Maximilian Kolbe) that each of us is accompanied by the grace of God from the cradle to the tomb, many of us simply don't tune in to the abundant graces that surround us. E-mail, meetings, laundry, deadlines—life becomes a series of tasks to be done rather than a series of blessings to behold. To the extent that we fail to recognize God's grace in our lives, we also fall short of completing the mission God has given us. In other words, we fail to answer our call. The remaining chapters in this section briefly examine several of the blinders we experience that cause this unfortunate occurrence in our lives.

CHAPTER TWO

Compartmentalization

A widespread, if not universal, criticism of the way Christians practice their faith today is that devotional activities are separated from all our other pursuits. When we work, we work; when we play, we play; when we socialize, we socialize; when we rest, we rest; and when we pray, we pray. Our lives have become compartmentalized, and so has our faith. Are you guilty of fragmenting your life this way?

Do you only look for Jesus during the times you are focusing on your faith compartment? When you are in your work compartment or your play compartment or any other compartment, do you fail to look for him because you're not in your faith compartment? The reality is that if you're not looking for him, it's unlikely you'll ever see him.

Former President Bill Clinton once told Oprah Winfrey that compartmentalizing led to his affair with intern Monica Lewinsky, describing "the costs of leading walled-off, parallel lives."[4] Our goal, of course, is the opposite: to be totally integrated, so that one aspect of our life jives with another, so what we profess on Sunday morning corresponds with how we behave on Saturday night. Rather than treat our faith like a compartment of our life, we should allow it to become the organizing and animating passion in all we do. Only then will we bring an abundance of miracles into our life.

Throughout history there may be no better example of a people who organized their lives and lived passionately in the presence of Jesus than the

Celts. The Celts were not subject to the blinders of compartmentalization because they viewed God as being an integral part of their lives and their world. At the heart of Celtic spirituality was the idea that God is present in some way in all things natural: rolling hills, bubbling brooks, blooming flowers. They also believed him to be present in animals: horses, chickens, cows, and newborn sheep. And perhaps most important, they believed him to be present in people: each and every one of us.

Celtic spirituality is down to earth. But in its elegant simplicity it is also deeply mystical. At its root is the magnificent mystery of the Incarnation: God became man and remains man and is still living with us today.

Celts cherish the story about the woman from Kerry who was asked where heaven is. She replied: "About a foot and a half above my head."

To a true Celtic believer, God is literally everywhere—certainly close enough to experience at any time. For such people it made little sense to look for God. They had only to open their eyes in the morning to greet him and their ears to hear him, their mouths to taste him and sing about him, and their minds to contemplate him. And they realized God even when it was only to fight or curse him!

Many of us, even though we belong to a community of modern-day believers, have lost touch with this robust type of spirituality. Secular society conditions us to be insensitive to the presence of God surrounding us in our daily lives.

The result is that we are like the disciples on the road to Emmaus—disappointed and disillusioned by the loss of our connection to God. And like those disciples, we fail to recognize that God is present at the same time we lament the lost connection.

Matthew Manion, CEO of the Catholic Leadership Institute in Pennsylvania, often refers to Salesian spirituality, named after the French bishop, St. Frances de Sales, which recognizes God's presence in everyday life. He tells the story of complaining to his spiritual director that he was feeling disconnected from God and was experiencing a spiritually dry time. After his second child was born, life got busier and he no longer felt he had the time for Bible study at his parish or quiet time with the Lord in Eucharistic Adoration.

His spiritual director challenged him to see God in his everyday life, not just in Adoration or the Bible. He challenged Matt to worship God in the splendid gift of creation that was his tiny baby. He encouraged him to use the bleary-eyed 3:00 A.M. feedings as a time to pray and reflect on God's presence in the bond between a parent and child and how that selfless love is only a shadow of the Father's love for us.

From that point on parenting became a prayer, and each moment Matt spent with his children was an opportunity to worship and connect with the Creator.

God is close, and his miracles are everywhere. He is with each of us on the road we must travel through life. He can work miracles for us every day if we merely recognize his presence and allow him to be part of our lives. The key is to use our free will to organize our lives and our thinking around his presence so he can be the driving force behind all our passions.

CHAPTER THREE

Ego

A popular explanation for the word "ego" is to present it as an acronym. E-G-O stands for "**E**dging **G**od **O**ut."

Edging God Out and putting yourself first means believing that all of your accomplishments are achieved *without* God's help.

Where did all your gifts come from? Who bestowed upon you all these gifts that allows you to achieve these things, anyway?

There's nothing wrong with respecting oneself. In fact, it's one of the things Jesus demanded of us. But there is a difference between respecting oneself and the uniqueness God gave each of us, and getting carried away to the extent that we think we can do it all without his help.

You should attack the blinders of ego on two levels: first on the individual level, then on the level of community.

Ego at the Individual Level

When the blinders of ego create problems for us as individuals, it usually happens because we are defining ourselves in terms of what we have accomplished rather than who we are. There is a huge difference between defining yourself in terms of your achievements (what you've done) rather than in terms of your life's calling (who you are). When people talk about their achievements, it's usually "all about me." Listen to the words they choose: "I did this," "I accomplished that," and so on. On the other hand, when people talk about who they are or what they perceive their calling to be, the words are different: "I'm a person who believes" or "I care about." Which perspective positions the person closer to God?

Stop and think about which category you fall in. What is your response when someone asks what you've been up to? How do you compose a Christmas letter summarizing the past year?

The best way to overcome the blinders of ego is to first have the humility to understand that God's will is different from your will. Then you must clearly define your call in life, relate it to God, and ask yourself whether you are living your life every day in accordance with your call.

The trap many of us fall into is defining our life's purpose by what we want to achieve and then to determine our self worth by evaluating our accomplishments. We focus on what we want to have and then think about what we need to do in order to get what we want. If we have any time left over, then we think about the persons we were created to be. The problem today is that the world is filled with too many human *doings* and not enough human *beings*. Even worse, we often evaluate ourselves in terms of what *others* think or say about our material accomplishments. You are much more than a resume, a series of bullet points and active verbs.

You should continually think about what you want your legacy to be. You should regularly ask, "What is my life's calling, given the gifts God has given me?"

Then, rather than thinking in terms of how you will *leave* that legacy, you should think in terms of how you will *live* that legacy, every moment of every day. Mother Teresa served as a striking example in recent times. She left a great legacy because she lived a great legacy. In fact, that's a statement we can make about all the saints.

Each of us has the potential to do the same. The key is to define and respond to your calling in life and not be trapped into thinking achievements are more important. *The necessary achievements will accrue if the calling is clear.*

But an even more exciting finding awaits you if you focus on calling versus achievement. You'll find that in the realm of achievement, there is little difference between "big" and "little" achievements. In fact, the little achievements often matter more in our daily lives than the big ones. When you truly understand your calling, you'll be afforded the opportunity to create "moments of magnificence," not only in your own life, but also in the lives of others. Consider the following story.

Years ago a man was flying home from the East Coast to San Diego one Friday evening and waiting to change planes in the Dallas airport. As he waited at the gate for his connecting flight to arrive, he couldn't help but notice a young mother and her two children under the age of five who were also waiting for the same plane. The kids were loaded with energy—supercharged, in fact. It didn't take long to learn why they were so hyped up. Their daddy was arriving on the plane on which the man would be departing. Every time a plane taxied by the gate, the kids would charge up to the windows, plaster their hands and cute little faces against the glass, and yell, "Is that Daddy's plane?" "Is Daddy here?" while jumping up and down in hopeful anticipation.

Finally Daddy's plane pulled in to the gate. Their energy level soared even higher, if that were possible.

Soon the passengers departed. Daddy, wearing a suit and carrying a briefcase, finally came through the door. The kids broke free from their mother and dashed over to Daddy. Each locked onto a leg, hugging Daddy vigorously while hopping up and down with glee. Daddy could barely move.

Then Mommy started over toward Daddy with a pleasant glow, accented with a loving smile.

When she was about five feet away, Daddy looked up at her, glanced at both her hands, and said, "Where's my coat? You forgot my coat."

The traveler watching this felt as though his heart had been broken into a million little pieces. Here was an opportunity for that father to create a true moment of magnificence, and he blew it.

Then the traveler started thinking. "How many times have I done the same thing? How many times has God given me an opportunity to bring a special moment of caring or happiness into the life of another and I've botched it because I was caught up in my own ego or sense of self-importance?"

His flight to San Diego was miserable—not because he was angry at that father for his insensitivity, but because he was terrified that he, too, shared some of that daddy's shortcomings. He recalled the many times he had let his ego get in the way of fulfilling what he knew part of his life's calling should be, which is to be an instrument of love and peace for those around him.

A mistake most of us make from time to time is in believing that *only* the big things matter. And the big things *do* matter. Trips to Disneyland, family vacations, wonderful birthday celebrations, and other special events *are* important. It's just that they're not the *only* things that are important. But here's the news flash: *They're not more important than all the little things—the day-to-day interactions, expressions of caring and sensitivity, and acts of thoughtfulness—that set the tone for your relationships and give ongoing meaning to your actions and your life.*

St. Josemaria Escriva penned the following thoughts regarding the little things:

Great holiness consists in carrying out the "little" duties of each moment.

Do everything for love. In that way there will be no little things: everything will be big. Perseverance in the little things for love is heroism.

A little act, done for love, is worth so much.

Do you really want to be a saint? Carry out the little duty of each moment: do what you ought and put yourself into what you are doing.[5]

There is no substitute for creating moments of magnificence at every opportunity. You should each make it part of your life's calling to do the little things that count. All day. Every day.

Ego at the Community Level

The second level upon which the blinders of ego must be attacked is on the level of community. Society plays a role in shaping our collective attitudes and beliefs. For the past several decades, society has been fixated on the supremacy of the individual, which in turn has fueled the dominance of ego. This spawned what has been called the era of rampant individualism. The norm for society in general has been to put self first. Especially during the 1980s and 1990s, selfishness and self-centeredness were seen as normal, acceptable, and even desirable by most of society. They have been variously labeled the "me" decades or the "I" decades because of the selfish and self-centered behaviors that characterized society in general during those times. These attitudes toward self-gratification reached their peak during the final years of the century just passed, where prurient, self-serving behavior was the acceptable norm.

Now, except for the brief period of time immediately following the terrorist attacks of 9/11, that trend has continued into the twenty-first century.

Jesus only gave us one commandment: "Love one another; even as I have loved you" (John 13:34).

In fulfilling this commandment, you should fight daily to cast off the blinders of ego by helping to build a culture of respect in every community of which you are a part. You should lead by your example in family, among friends and neighbors, and with colleagues and coworkers or fellow students. Your example should include putting community above self, placing respect for the dignity of others ahead of self-gratification, and demonstrating love above all.

CHAPTER FOUR

Disappointment

For many of us, it happens slowly, subtly, as part of growing up. Some might say it is part of the socialization process we experience as we mature. We lose our innocence and our naïveté. It starts when we learn that there's no Easter Bunny and that Santa Claus is a phony. Then we slowly discover that *God's* world—the one we learned about in our early religion education classes—is different from *our* world.

God's world is characterized by backlit saints and winged angels. In his world it is always easy to identify the good people from the bad and to side with the good ones.

But our world is different—more confusing, to say the least. We can't always recognize the saints and angels. Good people sometimes cause pain and hurt. The suffering is real and immediate, not just something we hear or read about from which we can easily escape. Then there are all the truly bad people who cause even greater hurt.

From time to time we find ourselves in painful situations, and it seems like there's no escape. And when we turn to him, sometimes our prayers are not answered in the way we'd like. Rarely are they answered immediately.

When we call out and we don't get an immediate and fully gratifying response, we start looking elsewhere. Before long, we look elsewhere so much that we stop looking in God's direction. We stop looking for him in our daily lives—and when we stop looking, we stop seeing.

When we stop seeing, we forget. We forget that God is there, whether we recognize him or not. The more we overlook his presence, the less able we are to recognize him in our lives. Then the worst happens—we begin to assume he is not there.

The story of the travelers on the road to Emmaus begins with their disappointment. They are blind to Jesus's presence on the road with them because they are overwhelmed with the events of the previous week. They were disciples—followers of Jesus's vision—and were devastated by the knowledge that Jesus had been crucified, died, and was buried. Then, to make things even worse, His body had disappeared from the tomb.

With the disappearance of Jesus's body, much of the hope, excitement, and faith shared by the disciples also disappeared. In their words, "We had hoped that he was the one to redeem Israel" (Luke 24:21).

The disciples' disappointment at the death of Jesus isn't much different from the disappointment many of us experienced as we grew up. The major difference is that theirs happened more suddenly as the result of a series of calamitous events that spanned less than a week. Our disappointment evolved more slowly. In fact, in most cases it happened so slowly, through so many different events, and over such an extended period of time that most of us didn't even recognize it as disappointment. But indeed, there was a gradual erosion of the idealism and enthusiasm that paved the sidewalks of our youth. We picked up subtle cues that the people around us didn't care as much as we thought they did or hoped they would—or maybe they don't care at all. We respond by mirroring their attitudes. This disappointment creates blinders that keep us from seeing the miracles of God's work in our lives.

Have you forgotten he is there? Have you stopped seeing him at work in your life?

The disciples' journey on the road to Emmaus is an apt metaphor for the spiritual journeys you must make as you travel through the pathways of your life. Just as the disciples' disappointment blinded them from Jesus's presence on their journey, your let downs can make you overlook the stardust of miracles in your own life. Jesus proclaimed, "The kingdom of God is at hand" (Mark 1:15): It is here, it is now, and we are in it.

CHAPTER FIVE

Tragedy

Our niece Melissa was eighteen when tragedy struck.

In June she had graduated as valedictorian of her high-school class. She had lots of friends because of her active involvement. She had been captain of the tennis team, class president, and homecoming queen—a vivacious teen with rosy cheeks and smiling eyes.

After a fun-filled summer she started studies at Claremont College where she quickly established a new circle of friends who were as bright, enthusiastic about life, and fun-loving as herself.

When she came home for Christmas, she was as content and excited as any eighteen-year-old could be. Her whole life was ahead of her—and what a grand life it promised to be.

The first night home she joined a group of her best friends from high school and they visited and reminisced until the early morning hours.

She hopped in a jeep with a several friends to head home, a short distance away.

A few blocks from home, in the middle of an upscale and tidy residential neighborhood, the drunk driver of another car careened down the street at eighty miles per hour, ran a stop sign, and smashed into the jeep. The driver of Melissa's car was killed instantly. Melissa was ejected, smashing the base of her skull into the nearby curbing. She died the next day. Another teen sustained permanently disabling injuries, and the other two passengers were seriously injured.

In the wake of this shock, many friends, relatives, and acquaintances landed on the same pointed question: "Where was God when this happened?"

* * *

It's an understandable question: bad things, good people, and a chasm that's hard to reconcile.

In the wake of 9/11, a small group of people went so far as to claim they knew the answer to this question, insisting that God was punishing Americans for our lapses in morality. In a September 13, 2001, interview on *The 700 Club,* Jerry Falwell said, "I really believe that the pagans, and the abortionists, and the feminists, and the gays and the lesbians who are actively trying to make that an alternative lifestyle, the ACLU, People For the American Way, all of them who have tried to secularize America. I point the finger in their face and say, 'you helped make this happen.'"[6]

When grief seizes our hearts and we give space to the doubts about God, our vision becomes narrowed by the blinders of tragedy. If God is in control, and God stands for goodness, then how can he let tragic things happen to his people?

Unfortunately, too many people answer this question by wrongly concluding one or more of the following:

- God is not in control.
- God is not present in our daily lives.
- The victims of tragedy were outside of God's will.
- The victims did something to deserve their tragic fate.

In other words, people tend either to dismiss God's presence entirely, or they accept his presence, but in a mean or vengeful context.

Although all these conclusions are incorrect, it's difficult to argue them with someone who is trapped in the throes of tragedy. That is why it is important for you to understand tragedy before it strikes.

There are three issues to come to grips with in order to put tragedy into perspective: (1) God gave each of us free will; (2) accidents happen; and (3) evil exists in the world.

One of the great mysteries of life is the mystery of free will.

The death of our niece Melissa is a striking example of the negative effects of free will coupled with bad judgment. The driver of the car that hit the teens' jeep used extremely bad judgment by drinking and smoking marijuana before getting behind the wheel of his car. In addition to killing three people and bringing crippling misery to their families, he also brought intense suffering to his own wife and children, one of whom had just been born.

The second important issue that defines our reality here on earth is that accidents happen. Sometimes these are the result of us exercising our free will, and sometimes they are simply accidents that happen without human initiative. They are just inexplicable accidents—catastrophic events that occurred and were not caused either by people or by God. A wrong turn, a gust of wind, a baseball that flies too fast and hits too hard.

And then, as 9/11 painfully demonstrated, there is a third source of despair in our world: tragedies resulting from evil.

The terrorists who struck on 9/11 were evil people. They had gone one step beyond the exercise of free will for self-gratification to a level where they actually wanted to kill other people and create destruction. Their actions were based on hate. In their purest and most simple form, these were evil people, driven to accomplish evil aims. Their acts were destructive and served no redeeming value to anyone.

The same can be said of serial killers, rapists, and any number of other people who are operating outside of God's will. They are the perpetrators of evil and the carriers of evil in our world. And they exist in all areas of the world.

So if God gave us a free will that we sometimes abuse through poor judgment, if accidents happen, and if evil exists in the world, where is God when innocent people become the victims of tragedy?

That's the question you must ask yourself (and encourage others to ask) every time tragedy strikes. Isn't that the message Jesus gives us in the following parable?

> As he passed by, he saw a man blind from his birth. And his disciples asked him, "Rabbi, who sinned, this man or his parents, that he was born blind?" Jesus answered, "It was not that this man sinned, or his parents, but that the works of God might be made manifest in him." (John 9:1–3)

When tragedy strikes, as part of dealing with our shock, grief, and dismay, one of the most important questions you should ask is, "Where is God at work in this?"

Rather than ask, "Why did God do this?" you should ask, "Where is he in all that is happening?"

Fr. John MacNamee, a poet and parish priest from Philadelphia, once commented, "The old die because they are old. The young die because they can. When someone dies tragically, we should not ask, 'Why did this happen? Why did God let this person die?' That question is not answerable in this life and will only frustrate us if we try to comprehend it. A better question to ask is, 'Why did this person live? And what can I learn from them in the way they lived their life? How can I honor them in the way I live mine?' That question can and should be answered by all affected by the tragedy. That is where we find God."

In the events of 9/11, the answers were abundant. Usually the greater the tragedy—meaning the more people affected—the more answers there will be. Can you think of other similar events that unveiled God's love? What about Hurricane Katrina, the California wildfires, the Haitian earthquake, or the Japanese tsunami?

The examples of heroism, charity, and compassion that people demonstrated for others during these catastrophes were almost endless. The shift in people's attitudes toward one another among those affected was noticeable and not limited only to the United States. People were nicer. They treated each other more politely and with greater respect.

In the case of 9/11, many people also changed their personal priorities. Americans quit jobs, quit whining, and quit waiting. They started school, started families, and started praying. Below is a comparison showing how Americans generally ranked eight core values before and after 9/11.[7]

	Rank before 9/11	Rank after 9/11
#1	Career	Family
#2	Heart	Heart
#3	Wealth	God
#4	Health	Health
#5	Home	Country
#6	Family	Home
#7	God	Career
#8	Country	Wealth

Even a cursory examination of these two lists shows God at work somewhere. Career and wealth went from #1 and #3, respectively, to #7 and #8. Family went from #6 to #1. And God moved from #7 to #3— certainly a move in the right direction.

Ask anyone if they noticed a general change in people's attitude and behavior toward other people in the wake of 9/11, and they will tell you they noticed a definite change in a positive direction. Sales of Bibles were up 38 percent in 2001 compared with 2000, with most of those sales occurring after 9/11.

The events of 9/11 brought families closer together, made friends and neighbors more appreciative of and respectful toward each other, and brought almost all of us closer to God. September 11, 2001, will become known as the historical turning point when our nation's underlying culture shifted away from self-centered individualism toward a more collaborative community epitomized by a general sense of positive spirituality and caring for the well-being of others.

When we suffer individual tragedy on a more personal level, the positive outcomes are not always so obvious and may not be nearly so profound. As a result we may not always see them as easily. Our grief may swallow them up, even if they were easy to identify without blinders.

But nonetheless, you should always trust in God. And the best way to demonstrate that trust is to ask, "Where is God with me in this?" Keep asking until the question is answered.

* * *

Stephanie Nielson was a doting mother of four, a green-eyed beauty in Mesa, Arizona, who delighted in entertaining friends and decorating her home—and who almost lost her life in a 2008 plane crash. She sustained burns over 80 percent of her body and saw a horrifying image reflected in the mirror. But she never let the blinders of tragedy narrow her vision, leaning on her faith in God to pull her through and chronicling the experience in a bestselling book called *Heaven Is Here: An Incredible Story of Hope, Triumph, and Everyday Joy*. It begins with a Louisa May Alcott quote about seeing clearly: "The power of finding beauty in the humblest things makes home happy and life lovely."

God doesn't abandon people just because an accident happened. He doesn't abandon people who are the victims of poor judgment or of evildoers. He is always there. It's up to us to find him.

God never changes. He always remains the same—infinitely loving, merciful, and kind. In teaching children about sin, we ask them to picture God as an anchor or an object that never moves. He is always the same in his glory, light, and grace. When we receive the sacraments, we move closer to him. When we sin, we move further away from his light. Unfaithfulness to him causes us to be vulnerable to the influence of the darkness. Only through the sacraments are we able to return to his heavenly light and goodness.

CHAPTER SIX

Modern Knowledge

Sometimes it seems as though the more we learn about our physical selves and the world around us, the more of an effort we make to confuse ourselves spiritually. We diagnose our outward symptoms on WebMd. com but overlook our inner lives. In many respects we spend a tremendous amount of intellectual energy creating a profound level of educated incompetence relating to things spiritual.

The latest example is in a new field of study that modern-day scientists have created and named "neurotheology." Neurotheology is the study of the brain's response to intense spiritual or mystical experiences. Some of the more publicized studies have involved the neuro-imaging and mapping of brain wave activity of both Tibetan Buddhists during intense meditative trances and Franciscan nuns during intense religious experiences. In both cases scientists were able to document profound increases in activity in the brain's prefrontal cortex. We know from previous studies that this means the subjects were focusing intently. At the same time the scientists were also able to observe and document almost a complete shutdown in activity of the brain's superior parietal lobe. This is the area of the brain that processes information about time and space and the body's relation to space. Taken together, we can conclude that during these intensely mystical experiences the subjects were keenly focused while functioning in a mental state that somewhat suspended their connection to self.

These are interesting findings, exciting to many. They have caused many believers to say, "Ha! I told you so." In other words, these maps of brain-wave activity are exactly what you'd expect during the course of deep and effective prayer—intense focus, yet grounded somewhere other than in self. These subjects have indeed found a way to connect with God.

Unfortunately, however, many neurotheologians have gone the opposite direction. They say it's our ability to create these specific patterns of brain functioning that cause us to believe in God. They argue further that a belief in God doesn't mean God exists, and that there is no evidence in their studies to show that God actually does exist. In essence, they are saying that God might merely be a figment of our imagination—an imagination that is steered in a particular direction because of special thoughts and feelings generated during certain types of meditation.

These theories are the spawning ground for many fervent discussions about our relationship to God. Is it the inner workings of our brain that cause us to incorrectly believe that a God exists? Or is it a true connection with God during these prayerful states that cause our brains to function this way?

Some would like us to believe that these dynamics, created in the inner workings of our brain, are what cause us to believe in a God that does not exist. In other words, God isn't real, but rather he is truly a figment of our imagination created very vividly by these altered mental states.

Books such as *Why God Won't Go Away: Brain Science and the Biology of Belief*[8] and *Zen and the Brain*[9] perpetuate the notion that it is the structure of our brain and our ability to manipulate this structure through meditation, prayer, or other intense emotional experiences that has caused people to believe in God.

In other words, these neuroscientists hold the view that many of the most fervent believers in God hold their beliefs not because they have experienced God firsthand because he truly exists, but rather because they manipulated their brains (or had them manipulated) in such a way as to create the illusion of God.

Some of these new neurotheologians claim to be taking an unbiased point of view by saying they are not taking sides in the argument. Their position is that our current knowledge doesn't allow us to draw a conclusion either way. They say that based on their studies we lack enough evidence to confirm either that our brain structures and processes create the idea of God or that God created our brain structures.

What an unfortunate and narrow view of the world, our lives, and everything around us!

This is but one example of the blinders created by our quest for more knowledge. It's not that knowledge or the quest for it is bad. Knowledge is good and so is its quest.

But since when does science give us permission to suspend our everyday reality and draw conclusions by only focusing on what appears on a cathode ray tube during a particular process, and totally ignore all the miracles that surround us? The quest for knowledge does not give us permission to ignore the valid experiences of our everyday lives.

How does what's happening inside a person's brain explain away all of God's magnificence and Jesus's everyday presence in our world?

We must be careful to avoid being drawn into irrelevant arguments that can be damaging to our psyches. By getting us to argue over whether or not our brains create the idea of God or God created our brains, these brain-mappers are subtly manipulating our thinking to get us to consider the premise that God does not, in fact, exist. This in turn fosters a mindset loaded with blinders that cause us to overlook Jesus's presence everywhere else.

If we experience the miracle of birth and the fierceness of thunderstorms, the song of a finch and the strength of an oak, we don't need to argue the existence of God or the presence of Jesus. We *know*.

It is not good science to study one aspect of our world—such as brain functioning during prayer—and then draw conclusions about our observations while ignoring all our other experiences. We must not abandon what we learn from our firsthand experiences. We must find comfort and have confidence in what we learn from these experiences. And we should nurture that comfort further by reminding ourselves daily to look for God and to recognize Jesus in everything we do. Once we realize again that he does, indeed, exist and is there for us, God is amazingly easy to find, and his miracles are easy to discover.

In this day and age, it's not enough merely to believe. We must nurture our beliefs and reinforce them at every opportunity. We must recharge them and revitalize them in order not to succumb to the continuous onslaught we will be subjected to as new knowledge and even newer levels of educated incompetence are developed. We must open our minds and our hearts, participating in the sacraments at every opportunity and letting their grace wash over us.

Reality is more a function of discovery than it is invention. As more and more people attempt to invent explanations that distort our reality, it is up to us to discover more examples of his true reality in our lives.

PART TWO

How We Lose Touch With Our Natural Gifts

Each of us encounters influences in life that are positive and others that are negative. Some of these influences help you become more aware of your natural gifts, while others can cause you to move away from or lose touch with your unique gift mix.

This section of the book identifies several factors that can work against you, often with your realizing. The best way to avoid negative consequences from these factors is to understand how they work and then to take steps to prevent their influence.

CHAPTER SEVEN

Influences From Significant Others

Tommy was eleven years old and loved football. He loved everything about it. He loved to watch it on television. He loved to read about it in the paper. He loved to talk about it with his friends. Most of all, he loved to play it—especially during football season. When he wasn't suited up and practicing or playing Pop Warner, he could be found someplace throwing or kicking the football with Teddy and Scott.

His second year playing Pop Warner promised to be even more exciting than his first. Joey, who was the team's star running back last year, would be moving up to an older division. That meant Tommy would have a shot at taking over the position this year. He had privately practiced his moves all summer long—sprinting from one corner of his backyard to the other, zigging and zagging, cutting and turning, stiff-arming imaginary tacklers, and spinning to break free from others until he was completely exhausted.

Then during the first game of the season, he received a handoff from the quarterback, broke through the line, and just as he was breaking free for a big gain—possibly a touchdown—he fumbled the football.

The coach was furious. He immediately sent in a substitute, called Tommy to the sidelines, and chewed him out. Among other things he said, "You'll never make a running back if you can't do something as simple as hold on to the ball when you run with it!" "How could you be so careless?" "Go sit over there on the bench and figure out whether or not you have what it takes to play football, because I don't think you do!"

Tommy was devastated. First, because he fumbled and second, because of the tirade from his coach. He'd seen professional football players fumble and they never got chewed out like that. In fact, a lot of times he saw their teammates and other people on the sidelines try to console them because they knew how bad it felt to fumble. Maybe Coach was angry because Tommy really didn't have what it takes. His confidence was shattered. He didn't want to go back in the game and risk another episode like this. He didn't even want to be there.

* * *

For as long as John can remember, his parents wanted him to become a doctor. Some of the very first words he can ever remember understanding were, "Look at that! He's going to make a fine doctor someday."

As early as elementary school, his parents were already discussing where he would go to college, and the discussion was always limited to only those universities that boasted the finest medical schools.

The problem was that John had always wanted to be a teacher. He was blessed to have experienced many fine teachers throughout his schooling and he admired the work they did, their dedication to helping their students learn, and the caring way they listened. He liked them so much that when he and his neighborhood friends played make believe, they always played school and little Johnny was always the teacher.

John made it through college and got into medical school, mostly because that's what his parents wanted. But after he graduated and started practicing, he became more and more miserable. He finally turned to alcohol as a way of easing the pain he experienced from being caught in a bind between what he felt called to do and a career path that entrapped him.

* * *

In order to understand how messages from other people influence your behavior, you must first acknowledge that you are ultimately responsible for how you behave. But what controls your behavior over time? What regulates your personal choices about how you act? Why do some people develop certain patterns of behavior different from others? During the past several decades psychologists and other experts in the field of human behavior have established one simple and indisputable fact: *Your image of yourself regulates your behavior over time.* In other words, more than anything else, who you think you are will determine how you act. There is truth to the age-old axiom, "As I think, therefore I am."

How many people do you know (or maybe you are one of those people) who are perfectly good communicators in one-on-one situations yet think they can't speak effectively to larger groups? The basic skills of articulation and verbalization are the same in both situations, so it isn't a question of ability. But because they *think* they aren't so effective in the large group, they don't perform as well.

Angela Baraquio knew she had to believe she could be crowned Miss America before a panel of judges would award her the title. The cradle Catholic from Honolulu was given a piece of advice from a former Miss Hawaii before she departed for the Atlantic City competition in October 2000: "I wish I had realized sooner I could have won." In other words, if you don't realize you've got a chance until the end of the pageant, it's too late. You must arrive with confidence. You must trust you have what it takes before you step onto the stage. Angela did, and she sparkled when became the first Asian American to be named Miss America.

On a smaller scale, you can see this played out on the fairway. Most golfers have an image—oftentimes based on past performance—of themselves as a particular kind of golfer. Once established, that image will go a long way to regulate a golfer's ongoing performance. If the golfer is playing worse than usual on a given day, there's a very good chance the golfer will have a few better-than-normal shots toward the end of the day. ("See, I knew I wasn't that bad.") Along the same line, if a golfer is having an exceptionally good day—playing well above his or her usual—then it's a pretty safe bet that the last few holes won't be played so well. ("It never fails. That's just the way I play!")

The only way to sustain changes in your behavior is to first change your image. When your mind envisions an image of yourself that it believes to be valid, that image will drive your behavior over time. Behavior conforms to image. When the two are out of alignment (for example, when your golf performance is better or worse than your image), then tension will grow in your subconscious mind until alignment is restored. The greater the difference between your image and your behavior, the greater will be the tension to eliminate the difference. Unless you change your image—a choice most people avoid—you can't hope to sustain changes in your behavior.

Another way to picture this dynamic is to imagine a set of scales with your image on one side and your behavior on the other, as shown in figure 7.1. If an imbalance occurs between your image of yourself and your behavior, the imbalance will create tension until balance is restored. The direction of the imbalance doesn't matter, but the magnitude does. The greater the discrepancy between your image and your behavior, the greater the tension you will experience until balance is restored.

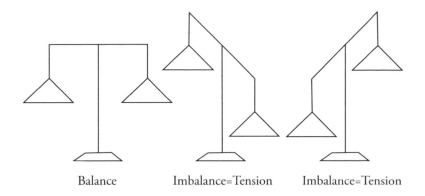

Balance   Imbalance=Tension   Imbalance=Tension

Figure 7.1 Tension When Behavior is Out of Balance

The tension people experience when there is a discrepancy between their behavior and their image often leads to even more overt emotions, such as embarrassment. An example of this could be the person who is not a heavy drinker, but goes to a party, drinks too much, gets drunk, and acts foolishly. The next day the person remembers (or finds out from others) what happened and becomes extremely embarrassed. Unless the person is an alcoholic (which is a different issue), that embarrassment, and all the other tension that is created along with the behavioral discrepancy, will cause the person to act more normally at the next party. The person might avoid drinking altogether at the next opportunity just to prove "I'm not that way."

If the regulator of our behavior is our self-image, how do we change our image?

You change your image through self-talk. Self-talk is how you talk to yourself about yourself. This is something you do all the time, often without realizing it. What you say about yourself shapes the way you think about yourself. All the little messages you send have a cumulative effect in

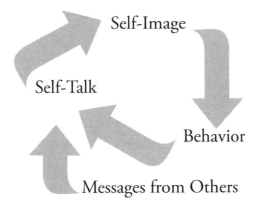

Figure 7.2 How Self Talk and Self Image Shape Personal Behavior

shaping your self-image. How you react to your behavior, how you react to the things other people say about you, and simply how you describe yourself all have the effect over time of shaping your image of yourself.

Figure 7.2 shows how this all comes together in a logical way. Your self-image drives your behavior. You respond to your behavior or things you've heard from other people with self-talk that in turn shapes your self-image

Therefore, the best way to sustain changes in your behavior is to change your image. If you change your behavior without changing the image, the change won't last because tension will be created that will cause the behavior to realign with the image.

The way to change your self-image is to program your self-talk.

Sometimes, though, we allow other people to program our self-talk for us. This is especially true if we see someone as having particular credibility because of his or her role or the special relationship that individual has with us. Parents, grandparents, teachers, clergy, coaches, and supervisors all have special roles that afford them the potential to significantly impact a person's self-talk, thereby altering that person's image and subsequent behavior. Depending upon our relationship and the credibility we give that "significant other" in our lives, this could be incredibly helpful or incredibly harmful. We've all heard stories of people who succeeded because someone close to them believed in them and that belief eventually overpowered the individual's self-doubts and lack of confidence to pave a pathway to success. When Michael Phelps became the most decorated Olympian in history, he credited his mother and Bob Bowman, the coach he's had since boyhood.

Unfortunately, more often than not, the reverse is true. We often allow negative messages from significant others to rein in our potential and not optimize our natural gifts. Teachers who say, "You will never be good at math"; coaches who say, "You just don't have what it takes"; and parents who ask, "Why are you such a bad child?" all run the risk of causing permanent damage. What determines whether or not these messages cause permanent damage is how they are interpreted through the receiver's self-talk and whether or not the messages change what the person believes to be true about him or herself. If the student says, "The teacher is a math expert and must know my math potential; therefore, I won't ever be good at math," then the damage is done. If the athlete reasons that the coach knows almost everything about sports and people's potential, then he or she might reasonably conclude, "I really don't have what it takes" and throw in the towel. The same could happen with the child who concludes, "My parents are always telling me I'm bad. They must know. Therefore, I must be bad."

Children and young people are more susceptible to having their self-image changed by the talk of others, but adults are not completely immune. We've all seen someone who loses confidence because of feedback that was improperly given. We've also witnessed events that created a cataclysmic effect on a person's image. A common example is when a person stumbles over a word while giving a speech and concludes that he or she will never be a good speaker.

All of this can be diagrammed as shown in Figure 7.2.

The key to avoiding the negative messages from significant others to inappropriately influencing your self-image is to inoculate yourself by carefully thinking through the messages you allow to program your self-image. Never accept a negative comment from someone else about you without careful discernment.

Therefore, the key to achieving sustained positive performance or behavior is to manage your self-talk. Here's the process you should follow:

1. Decide what you want your performance or behavior to be.

2. Make statements about yourself in positive, present-tense language, *as if the changes have already been achieved.*

3. Repeat those statements regularly and make sure that the positive assumptions are reflected in all other statements you make about yourself.

Let's examine an example from personal experience. Years ago when Dick was in college, he started smoking. He quickly became a regular smoker, smoking at least half a pack a day. He took the habit with him into the Navy after being commissioned as a Naval Officer. After a few years he decided to quit. Every time he tried to quit, though, he changed his behavior without changing either his self-talk or, most important, his self-image. When people would offer him a cigarette, he'd say, "No, thanks. I'm trying to quit." Think about what this message says. It says, "I'm a smoker who's trying to quit." If a person's image is that he or she is a smoker trying to quit, then how must that person act in order to eliminate any tension between behavior and image? The person must first smoke; otherwise, he or she can't try to quit. Next the individual must *try* to quit without actually quitting, because once the person quits he or she can no longer try.

Therefore, if you want to quit smoking, what is the key? It is to talk about yourself as if you're a nonsmoker and to not smoke. So if someone offers you a cigarette, your answer should be, "No, thanks. I don't smoke." Every time you say that about yourself, you reinforce your image of yourself as a nonsmoker. Eventually it becomes harder for you to smoke, because you believe and think about yourself as a nonsmoker, *rather than as a smoker who's trying to quit.*

The same thing happens to those who try to lose weight—or who try to do anything, for that matter. *People who try, try; people who do, do.*

So, how do you make this work for *you*

- First, set goals for yourself. *(Get rid of twenty pounds.)*
- Translate your goal into a positive, present-tense statement, as if it were already achieved. *(I weigh 160 pounds and look and feel great.)* It's okay to have more than one such statement. *(I eat only the healthy foods I need to maintain my weight at 160 pounds; I exercise regularly so I can keep my weight at 160 pounds.)*
- Write these positive, present-tense statements on cards that you carry with you, and *read and repeat them whenever possible.* Each time you repeat them, you will be programming your self-image to create tension that will pull your behavior in the right direction.
- When you refer to yourself in all your other conversations, make sure you refer to yourself *as if these statements were true.* (For example, "No, thanks; I don't smoke," even though you may still be in the throes of quitting.)
- Ensure that you filter the things other people say about you through the lens of your positive, present-tense statements. If someone says or implies something about you that is contrary to your statements, you

should rebut it *in your own mind.* There's no need to get into a big argument with them about what's true and what isn't. Simply say to yourself, "That's not me. Even though that person's perception may be real to them, it's not valid as far as I'm concerned. *This* is who I am."

- Revisit your goals and statements regularly to ensure they are aligned. Rewrite different statements if necessary to freshen them and add vitality on a regular basis.

Perhaps the most important thing to remember regarding self-talk is that you should audit yourself on a regular basis to make sure the things you say *and imply* about yourself reinforce the image of the person you want to be. "As I think, I am," is a fundamental truism. The way you control how you think about yourself is to control how you talk about yourself.

Matt Manion from the Catholic Leadership Institute offers an interesting perspective on how we view input from others as we attempt to get in touch with our unique gifts and abilities. He uses the concept of the social mirror.

The social mirror is simply what we know about our gifts and talents based on what others have reflected back to us. We hear observations such as, "Joe is really good with numbers." "Sonji is not very athletic." "Juan is a talented singer." From these observations we begin to develop a picture of ourselves and our gifts.

The risk in listening *exclusively* to the social mirror is that people can reflect back to us only what they have already observed in us. They cannot see the untapped potential or gifts that lay dormant within us. The challenge is to be informed by the social mirror but not blinded or limited by it. If God placed a passion, drive, or desire in our heart, we should pursue that. We should live from our imagination and dream of what can be and not focus exclusively on what has been.

Pat DeAngelis had a desire to be a nurse. From an early age she wanted to bring the healing compassion of Christ to those who suffer. After high school, Pat applied to nursing school and was rejected. She applied to another nursing school and was rejected again. However, she was determined to pursue her passion. Pat was rejected from eight nursing schools before finally pleading with the admissions officer at a ninth school that she had to be a nurse and couldn't imagine herself in any other profession. Moved by her determination, the admissions officer let her in.

Pat not only thrived in nursing school, but she also went on to have a thirty-year career in healthcare. Today she is president and CEO of a leading community hospital. If you ask Pat what has motivated her all along, her answer remains unchanged: She wants to bring the compassion of Christ to every patient in her hospital. Pat refused to allow the negative feedback from the first eight admissions officers keep her from her unique life's purpose. As a result, she was rewarded with a fulfilling and successful career.

* * *

One of the biggest challenges in developing our natural gifts is not being swayed by the negative influences of others. The most meaningful goals in life are those that can only be accomplished with the help of God's graces. We should use those graces to give us confidence that, with God's guidance and help, our gifts are capable of being developed well beyond our imagined potential. Through him all things are possible.

CHAPTER EIGHT

Education

Unfortunately, the formal education process in most countries is more a process of socialization than it is a process of developing individual human potential. Numerous studies have shown that there is little or no correlation between class standing (or grade point average in college) and a person's success after graduation. In fact, several studies have actually demonstrated an inverse correlation. People at the bottom of their class academically generally achieve greater success (at least measured extrinsically) than those at the top.

The most tragic aspect of the education process takes place when the process divorces individuals away from their true gifts—when a person's potential (or gift mix) is diminished because their aptitude, interests, and natural abilities are outside the boundaries of the educator's focus. Students quickly learn there is something wrong with them or they are less of a person if they don't fit the mold like everyone else. As a result, they stop using their gifts. When they stop using them, they stop developing; when they stop developing, they fall far short of true fulfillment.

Buckminster Fuller once noted that we are all born geniuses and society de-geniuses us. It's up to each of us to not allow this to happen.

We all have different natural gifts bestowed upon us by God. The only valid measure of success in life is whether or not we develop our gifts to their fullest potential, use them in a way that brings glory and honor to God and touches people in a special way. For many of us this means overcoming the negative aspects of socialization that are imposed upon us by the process of formal education.

Take a minute to recall your earliest ambitions, the life your five-year-old self envisioned in unrestricted terms. Astronaut? Clown? Priest? Painter? What would you do if you'd never seen the paint-by-numbers? What color would you choose? So often the fundamentals that bring us joy and freedom in childhood remain unchanged over the decades.

CHAPTER NINE

Path-Determinate Choices

When he graduated from college, Jeremy still hadn't decided what he wanted to do for a career. In fact, he hadn't thought much at all about his career. All he knew was that he was tired of not having enough spending money to do the things he really enjoyed. Like a lot of young men from southern California, he liked to surf and spend time at the beach. He enjoyed most sports, including golf, and he liked to go camping and fishing. He also wanted a new car—an SUV. In reality, that would give him comfortable access to the kind of lifestyle he craved.

When it came time to look for a job, Jeremy was most concerned about finding something that gave him reasonable spending money, left him free on the weekends, and didn't require him to go back to school. His undergraduate degree was in business, and he had toyed with the idea of going on to earn a master's degree in business administration—but not for very long. He could always go back and pick that up if he needed it. Right now, though, he wanted to enjoy life more.

After searching for a while, he found that the easiest jobs to get were in sales. The base salaries were higher than any job had paid him to date, and with the commissions and incentive plans that went along with sales jobs, some looked pretty enticing. It didn't take long for him to find one he liked. He took the job, learned and performed well, and easily settled into his new lifestyle. He rented an apartment near the beach with a few of his college buddies and basked in the warmth of the sun and contentment.

Five years later, however, discontentment started to creep up on Jeremy. Even though he was doing the things he had always enjoyed, mostly with people he liked, he felt as if he were in a rut. "You're finally realizing that you have to grow up sooner or later," his brother told him one day when they were returning from a camping trip. "There's certainly nothing wrong with a career in sales," his brother explained. "The problem is that you don't know if that's what you want. You're feeling trapped because you've worked your way to the top of the commission and bonus structure; if you change jobs, you'll lose all those perks you've built up. You're afraid to go back to school because you don't want to take even a temporary step backward. But most important, you don't have a clue about what you want to do with your life."

* * *

Jeremy's problem, like that of so many young people in his generation, is that he allowed himself to be boxed in by path-determinate choices. In other words, past choices he made about his career and his calling are now determining what options he might have in the future. His situation is very much like the nursing student who decides in her final year of nursing school that she doesn't want to be a nurse. It's difficult, to say the least, to try to change sentiments at the last minute and seek a job doing something else.

It's hardest for trained professionals to choose a different path than the one they determined years ago before they started training. Consider the doctor, lawyer, or accountant who chose to enter a specific profession in early college or high school for reasons other than a direct knowledge of what the work itself would be like. They become miserable actually doing the work years later when the chosen career actually starts.

Some path-determinate choices have to do with schooling. "I trained six years to be a doctor. I can't waste all that money, time, and effort to do something else now." Others have to do with on-the-job training. "I've been learning this job for the past three years; it would be foolish for me to walk away from it." Still others have to do with seniority ("I've invested all this time accruing tenure"), benefits ("I'm at the top of my scale here, why would I want to start all over somewhere else?"), or perceived disadvantage ("I'd be way behind everyone else doing that; I'd be starting at the bottom of the learning curve"). But regardless of the source of concern that tends to lock a person into a predetermined path that may not be optimal, one thing is certain: The more trapped a person becomes, the more separated that person will become from his or her natural gifts.

Gimmicky articles listing the best-paying careers lure wayward job seekers whose discernment should be based on their passions, not their paychecks. Most original path-determinate choices people make are not made on the basis of a person's unique gift mix. They are made on the basis of: immediate gratification ("I can earn money now"), comfort ("This is an easy place to go to school"), or extrinsic factors ("Salespeople make lots of money") as opposed to, "I really love to serve people with my selling skills." This can be fine for the short term. It can become a huge problem later on, however, when a person realizes that the path has become a rut from which they can't seem to escape. It's as if our feet are bound by rubber bands to the path we're on. We stick to the familiar: the same parking pass, the same faces, the same email address, the same retirement plans.

Short-term choices that set a person on a particular career path are fine as long as those choices are recognized for what they are. When decisions made to satisfy short-term or immediate criteria start to dictate long-term decisions that should be evaluated according to completely different criteria, frustration is inevitable. Even more serious, we set ourselves up to fall short of our potential.

Teresa Crowe is an impressive young Catholic who was once boxed into path-determine choices. She wrote about her experience jumping outside:

It may seem foolish to keep a terrible job, but there are many reasons to do so. I know them well. There's the power of a paycheck. The dictates of a framed diploma. The weight of others' expectations. And the command of the status quo. These things kept me going for many months. My expensive engineering degree from Duke had landed me on a prescribed career path in an in-demand industry, a position many of my peers envied.

But I was miserable. I spent eight or nine hours a day on the computer, largely removed from human contact.

Sure, I was good at engineering, but I had always viewed it as one part of my life; it was beginning to take up all my time and zap all my energy.

Deep down, I knew what I wanted to do. I wanted to teach. But the prospect of leaving my job and starting over freaked me out.[11]

Teresa brought all those anxieties to a weekend retreat, waking Sunday morning with a sense of peace and the resolution to start applying for teaching positions. But come Monday morning, behind the wheel on her commute to work, all those familiar worries and what-ifs returned. Suddenly a commercial came on the radio broadcasting a Catholic schools job fair being held nearby in two weeks. She attended, and she got a job.

Teresa is now in her eighth year teaching. "There is no doubt in my mind that I am living my vocation and doing what I am meant to be doing," she wrote. "Teaching is exhausting, but when I crawl into bed each night, I feel truly fulfilled. What more could you ask for?"

Each of us should take time out periodically to assess the path we're following in life, especially with our careers. Ask the following questions:

- Are the reasons I chose this path still valid? In other words, if I were to start all over today, would I still pursue this path for my career?
- What has changed since I started on this path (both for me and my family)?
- What have I learned about my true passion and my natural gifts since I started down this path?
- If there is another career path that I would find more fulfilling and think it would be a better fit with my natural gifts—and I assumed there was no way I could fail following that path—what is that path? What are the perceived constraints holding me back from moving in that direction?

These questions are a preview of the types of questions you'll be asked to answer in Part III. So if you can't answer all of them immediately, without reflection and introspection, don't worry. It's important for you to be able to distance yourself from some of the past and current assumptions about your current constraints if you are going to truly discover the full range of your natural gifts in preparing to fulfill your unique promise.

It's also essential that each of us explore our passions, our gifts, and our purpose *as we live our lives*, as opposed to locking ourselves into path-determinate choices that separate us from our purpose and prevent us from fulfilling our true promise.

CHAPTER TEN

Stagnation and Complacency

Sometimes we just become bored or burned out. After having worked with a number of people who are victims of career-related stress, we've pinpointed the more common cause: it's not that they've worked too hard, it's that they lack passion for what they're doing.

Stories abound of people who thrive on difficult, stressful work—they're actually energized by it—because they feel a sense of contribution and achievement. They know they made a difference. Hard workers who don't share these feelings are most often the first victims of burnout.

Often people wind up in this situation because they don't distinguish between their *job*, their *work,* and their *career.* A person's *job* consists of the role they play with their employer. It includes things like work hours, pay, benefits, relationships with other people in the company, and working conditions. A person's *work* consists of all the activities they perform while fulfilling this role, such as manufacturing things, taking care of customers, leading others, problem solving, decision making, planning— all the things a person does to contribute to the organization's results. A person's *career* is the purposeful path through life each person chooses in order to achieve fulfillment. For example, a person might choose a nursing career, a teaching career, a career as a homemaker, or a career in construction, manufacturing, sales, or marketing. Thus, a person might choose a *career* in the field of education, hold a *job* as a teacher, and do the *work* of teaching history to fourth graders.

Often when people are asked how they like their career, they respond by saying how much they like their job. The pay is pretty good, they say, the company provides good benefits, and the people are okay—all descriptions of a job, not a career. A person who answers the question this way is a sure candidate for burnout as well as becoming a victim of stagnation and complacency.

It's entirely different for someone to respond by talking about how much they are learning, how far they've progressed in the past few years, or how excited they are about a recent or pending accomplishment. People who answer the question in these terms also tend to be more closely in touch with their own natural gifts and how those gifts are developing. They can also probably explain in reasonably certain terms how they are contributing to the organization's success.

Contribution and development are the antidotes for stagnation and complacency. It's nice to have a "good job"—meaning all the extrinsic factors are in place and positive. Check, check, and check. But it's great to feel good about your work, the contribution you're making, and the progress you're experiencing on your chosen career path. Do you have a good job, or do you feel good about your job?

Ask yourself the following questions:

- *What is it about my current situation that I like?* If most of your answers focus on extrinsic factors such as working hours, pay, benefits, working conditions, and the like, then you are probably going to end up a victim of stagnation and complacency sooner or later. If most of your answers focus on the contribution you're making and the fulfillment you're experiencing, then you're probably not separating yourself from your natural gifts or your calling.

- *What is it about my current situation that I* don't *like?* There is a false perception that fulfilled people are never dissatisfied. That's not true. People who achieve fulfillment are frequently dissatisfied. The difference is that they are dissatisfied about the right things. It's okay to be dissatisfied with your current level of development; you should want to learn more and develop your gifts to the fullest. It's okay to be dissatisfied with your current performance and that of your organization; you should always want to do better. It's okay to be dissatisfied with the level of impact you are having on the world; you should always want the world to be better as a result of your contributions. Focus on getting it right, and the rewards (pay, benefits, and the like) will follow. Focus on getting rewards, and you'll never get it right.

When all is said and done, life is an evolutionary process. To evolve requires change. Once you stop evolving—which means you also stop changing—then you stop living. The only difference between a rut and a grave are the dimensions.

Some have defined insanity as repeatedly "doing the same things and expecting different results." When stated this way, the need to do things differently becomes painfully obvious. Yet it's amazing how many people don't do things differently yet continue to expect different results. This highlights the distinction between blind hope and optimism. Blind hope encourages people to do nothing to make things different. It encourages passivity and a reactionary lifestyle. "I'll just continue on the way I have been, hoping something different will happen." Optimism, on the other hand, encourages a proactive frame of mind, along with initiative. Optimism implies a creative force that stimulates action and change. "I'm confident that if we try this, good things are likely to result." An optimistic single person who feels called to marriage joins a dating site and invokes guidance from the Holy Spirit. A blindly hopeful single person rejects online dating and waits for a chance encounter like the ones scripted in Hollywood and acted by Drew Barrymore.

We should, therefore, be more optimistic than hopeful—more proactive than reactive—in order to win the battle against stagnancy and complacency. It is up to each of us to create our future and, ultimately, our legacy.

An esteemed colleague, Larry Wilson, is fond of saying: "If we always do what we've always done, we'll always get what we've always got."

PART THREE

How to Reconnect and Answer Your Call

One of our most important struggles in life is to overcome the blinders that separate us from God's graces and the negative influences that distance us from our natural gifts so we can answer and fulfill our call.

The chapters in this section explain all nine dimensions that must be addressed in order to do that. In a simple-to-follow format, they will guide you through a process for identifying your call and preparing a plan to fulfill it.

CHAPTER ELEVEN

Overcoming the Blinders and Influences

God's supernatural graces can only work in our lives if we first acknowledge God's presence and his miracles daily. We must consciously shed the blinders that separate us from him in order to benefit from his grace.

The most powerful force in the world today is prayer. Jesus said, "Ask and it shall be given to you, seek and you shall find, knock and it shall be opened to you" (Matthew 7:7, *NAB*). Christ himself went off into the desert to pray for forty days before beginning his public ministry. At numerous other times in the Gospels, he spent time alone in prayer. If Christ took forty days in prayer, how much time do you think you will need to spend in prayer to find and answer your call? There is no activity you can engage in that will have a greater guarantee of success. Therefore, to bring the miracles of God into your life each day, you should pray.

Cardinal Timothy Dolan of New York stressed this in a recent tweet. (Who doesn't love a cardinal on Twitter?) "Daily prayer," he wrote, "is the foundation of sanctity."[12]

Be persistent but sincere. Recognize that you are in the presence of God and think about what you are saying. Pray from your heart, speak slowly, and reflect upon your words. Don't simply repeat prayers you've memorized.

In addition to your usual devotions, set aside time each day for a prayer session. You might want to begin with the following prayer.

Prayer to the Holy Spirit
Come, Holy Spirit, enlighten my heart,
to see the things that are of God;
Come, Holy Spirit, into my mind,
that I may know the things that are of God;
Come, Holy Spirit, into my soul,
that I belong only to God.
Sanctify all that I think, say and do,
that all will be for the glory of God.
Amen.

Next, take a moment to remind yourself of God's presence in your life on this particular day. As St. Josemaria Escriva wrote:

It's necessary to be convinced that God is always near us. Too often we live as though our Lord were somewhere far off—where the stars shine. We fail to realize that He is also by our side—always.

For He is a loving Father. He loves each one of us more than all the mothers in the world can love their children; helping us and inspiring us, blessing...and forgiving.

We have to be completely convinced, realizing it to the full, that our Lord, who is close to us and in heaven, is a Father, and very much our Father.[13]

Think of all the things around you that God, in his infinite wisdom, has created. Recognize the miracles of his creation you have encountered: a sturdy old oak silhouetted against the sunrise, a rosy-cheeked grandchild perched at your feet; a hawk soaring overhead. Allow yourself to be amazed at God's creation.

And then give thanks. Raise your heart to God in true thanksgiving for the wonderful blessings he has allowed you to experience.

The word *miracle* comes from the Greek word *meidan*: "to smile." Miracles are meant to be enjoyed, beheld. So go ahead: Take it in, inhale deeply, and smile!

If you are in the midst of struggles or challenges, ask God, "Where are you at work in all this?" Think about ways you can turn those struggles into triumphs with God at your side.

Finally, ask for God's guidance. Without him we can do nothing of meaning. Ask for more than a mere relationship with God; ask for an intimate union with him. Trust him to show you the way. Ask him to make your life a prayer. Ask him to make everything you do each day—whether with family, friends, or coworkers—a prayer. In other words, even though you sometimes set aside specific times to pray, consider your entire life to be a prayer. Treat your work, family, and faith all as one, always, because you are in union with Christ, who is in you.

God's way is *the* way. Trust him by inviting him to play a conscious and deliberate role in your daily activities, and the miracles he will bring will come forth in abundance. And those daily miracles will eventually lead to the biggest and most important miracle of all: eternal happiness with him in heaven.

As you think about your purpose and promise, it is helpful to call on St. Joseph for guidance. Two prayers in particular can serve as meaningful guides to more effectively integrate faith, work, and family.

St. Joseph's Worker's Prayer
St. Joseph, example for all those who work to support themselves and their families, obtain for me the grace to labor with thankfulness and joy. Grant that I may consider my daily endeavors as opportunities to use and develop the gifts of nature and grace I have received from God. In the

workplace may I mirror your virtues of integrity, moderation, patience, and inner peace, treating my co-workers with kindness and respect. May all I do and say lead others to the Lord and bring honor to God's name. Amen.[14]

Prayer for One's Family
Heavenly Father, I thank you for the gift of my family and for the many joys and blessings that have come to me through each of them. Help me to appreciate the uniqueness of each while celebrating the diversity of all. Through the intercession of St. Joseph, foster father of your Son, I ask you to protect my family from the evils of this world. Grant us all the power to forgive when we have been hurt and the humility to ask for forgiveness when we have caused pain. Unite us in the love of your Son, Jesus, so that we may be a sign of the unity you desire for all humanity.
St. Joseph, intercede for us. Amen.[15]

Remember, today's world is beyond post-Christian, as many refer to it; it is *anti*-Christian. A failure to understand this weakens our ability to answer our call to God. In a September 2003 address to newly ordained bishops, Bl. John Paul II said, "Our time…is marked by confusion and uncertainty. Many people—even Christians—seem bewildered and devoid of hope."[16]

The way to combat all the anti-Christian influences in the world and stay close to God is to pray. To paraphrase St. Alphonse Liguori, people who do not pray will not be saved. If we are not on a path toward personal salvation, we'll never be able to lead others toward salvation. It should be easy for us to pray; we have so many real opportunities— such as participating in the Eucharist daily. It's up to each of us to avoid the commitments that clutter our calendars and our hearts, giving us an excuse to flee from an interior life. Fleeing from your interior life only results in a flight from God, and a flight from God is a flight that takes you away from your unique call on this earth.

Within this context there are four things you can do to overcome the blinders and influences:

- First, be extremely clear about your own three-dimensional call. You absolutely must know what you want to leave as your unique legacy.
- Second, live that legacy daily, remembering that the little things count most. Your beliefs and purpose should be reflected in everything you do.
- Third, project your faith outward. Remember the old axiom, "The best way to learn is to teach"? The same principle applies to your faith. One of the best ways to grow in your faith is to share it with others.
- The fourth and final step is to network with like-minded people. Get involved in your parish. Reach out to other Catholics. Join Catholic organizations that sponsor activities aligned with your interests. Create interdependent relationships with other Catholics so you can help answer each other's call.

If you faithfully follow these guidelines, you'll find yourself on a path that will accomplish two objectives. First, it inevitably will draw you closer to God and his graces. Second, it will inspire you to develop your personal gifts much more quickly in a way that will lead to the true fulfillment of your potential.

> The word of God is a light for our path. We must assimilate it in faith and prayer and put it into practice.
>
> —*CCC*, 1802

CHAPTER TWELVE

The Three Dimensions of Your Divine Call

Christians have long embraced the sacred mystery of the Blessed Trinity: God the Father, God the Son, and God the Holy Spirit united into one being. The foundation of our faith stems from the integration of these three as one.

During biblical times, numbers held great significance. Perhaps it was because of the Holy Trinity that the number three came to signify perfection, fullness, and completeness. Perhaps this is also why, when we think of perfection, wholeness, and completeness as human beings, we conclude that it has three components in one.

We can describe this human wholeness or completeness as being when a person:

1. combines his or her natural gifts
2. with God's supernatural grace
3. to fulfill that person's unique life purpose.

When all three come together, the result is some degree of human perfection, which can be shown in figure 12.1.

Your *call* is your potential to fully develop your personal gifts while combining them fully with God's grace to completely fulfill your unique purpose. The more you can expand the center area where the three components overlap with each other, the stronger your life will be, and the more fulfillment you will find. Ideal integration would be represented by a

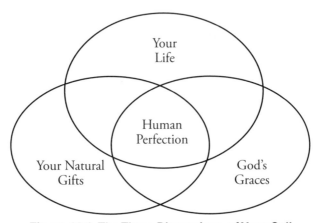

Figure 12.1 The Three Dimensions of Your Call

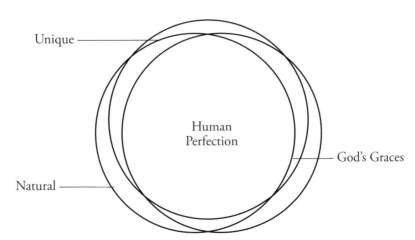

Figure 12.2 Approaching Ideal Integration

complete overlap. This is what the saints accomplished to achieve sanctity in their lives on earth. Although you may never be able to achieve complete integration, you should at least strive for something that represents the ideal as shown in figure 12.2.

To the extent that the number three had special significance in biblical times because it represented perfection, the number nine took on even more significance because it represented perfection multiplied by perfection. In fact, this is how the practice of praying novenas developed among Catholics. *Novena* is derived from the Latin word *novem*, which means nine. Novenas developed because Catholics believed that nine days was a perfect amount of time to pray. Therefore, it is fascinating to realize that each of the three elements of this overarching framework can be further divided into three more dimensions for a total of nine. This is what it all boils down to. Let's examine the purpose ring first.

The Three Components of Purpose

Each person's life purpose is characterized by three inseparable components that can best be understood through the example of St. Joseph. For more than 2,000 years, we've overlooked the true meaning of the example of the foster father of Jesus, Joseph of Nazareth. Throughout the ages Joseph has been referred to as a just and righteous man, close to God in every respect. He is variously referred to as a father, a spouse, the head of the Holy Family, a worker, a carpenter, and a man of great faith. All of these are correct, of course, but considered separately, they are incomplete. He was all of these, but what is most important is that he was all of these *at the same time!*

The roles he fulfilled can be grouped into three distinct categories: faith (as both a prayerful and faithful man who carried out God's will), family (as both spouse and parent), and external service to humankind (as a carpenter he provided for his family while building for others).

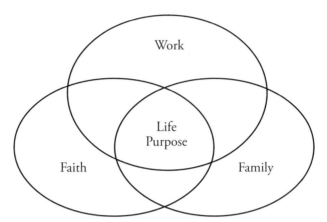

Figure 12.3 The Elements of Personal Purpose

A mistake we often make when thinking about our purpose in life is to think of it as being in one dimension. However, it is three-dimensional for everyone. We first must be faithful, honoring God in all we think and do. *At the same time* each of us has a call to be magnificent in our families (for the religious, their family is the Church) as spouse, parent, sibling, offspring, or extended family member. Likewise, *at the same time,* each of us has a call to the external world through the "work" we do (both paid and unpaid), a contribution we make to our faith communities, the communities in which we live, and the world at large through what we often refer to as our careers or vocations. Your purpose should never be limited to just one of these categories, nor should you trade one for the other. Your total life's purpose is all three, as shown in figure 12.3.

The more you can expand the center area where the three departments of your life overlap with each other, the stronger your life will be and the more fulfillment you will find. Ideal integration would be represented by a complete overlap. Although you may never be able to achieve complete

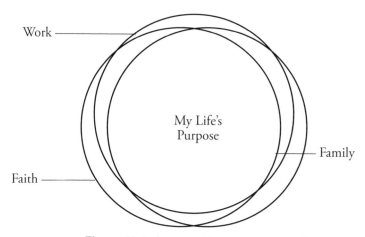

Figure 12.4 Approaching Ideal Integration

integration, you should at least strive for something that represents the ideal as shown in figure 12.4.

It's sad to see someone focus on one part of life at the expense of the other two. A colleague of ours once conducted an assessment of how much of his time he'd put into his family life, his social life, and his work life over the past ten years. Upon completing the assessment, he turned pale and looked as if he had been kicked in the stomach. This was the first time, he explained, that he had fully realized why his wife of twenty-two years had recently left him. For two decades he'd been an international consultant, traveling the world, spending a great deal of time away from home and directing a tremendous amount of his energy toward his clients. Most of the time he spent at home during that period was recharging his batteries—in other words, getting energy from his family but giving very little back. When he decided to take a sabbatical after twenty years, he took up lobster fishing to keep busy. This kept him out in his boat for long hours away from his family, still giving very little to them. When his wife finally threw in the towel, it was because the marriage had been lopsided the entire time. There was nothing more he'd like to do, he confided, with sadness dulling his eyes, than redo those past two decades so he could live a more balanced and integrated life, ultimately being a better spouse and father.

This doesn't mean that you can't have a career involving travel or separation from your family. It's possible *if* you understand your priorities and hold yourself accountable to those priorities. We are blissfully married in spite of being apart thirty-one of the first thirty-six months of our marriage due to Dick's military obligations. As a young naval officer, Dick completed two major deployments and two special missions to Vietnam, along with normal time at sea between those missions. Through letters and occasional phone calls, our relationship grew.

Upon leaving the Navy, Dick became a management consultant much like the colleague previously described. However, there were several major differences between our lifestyle and our colleague's. When Dick traveled, he stayed in close contact. Dick typically called home every night to talk to Martha and eventually to the kids. When Dick was home, the family spent quality time together. In fact, the case could be made that Dick spent more quality time with family and kids during that time than many of their friends and neighbors who didn't travel. Yes, many men they knew were home more than Dick. But plopping down in front of the TV every night and drifting into a mute, mindless zone is not the same as meaningful bonding with family. Spending six hours every weekend playing golf with the guys isn't the same as taking a day trip, a weekend trip, or even completing some special project with the family.

One summer, as a family we spent every available moment building a three-story tree house in a giant oak tree on their property. It had a sliding pole, a retractable staircase, a basket, and pulley that went up thirty-five feet to the third story—this was one amazing tree house. Our kids are all adults now, but they still remember the time our family spent that summer building the tree house and the many nights they spent sleeping in it. Friends saw the tree house and asked when we ever had time to build it, given how involved we were with career, church activities, school, and community events. The answer, of course, is that finding the time wasn't hard because family was always an equal priority.

We also integrated family time with career time. For example, when Dick had clients in Australia and New Zealand, we took major family vacations to both countries. Our children still remember those as some of the most fun and fulfilling times we spent as a family. They say the same about Hawaii, Washington, D.C., and Europe.

The point is that career, family, and faith were never separate for us. It's one of the reasons why our eldest daughter, Jennifer, developed such a passion for travel and realized her natural gifts as a teacher. It helped our second daughter, Whitney, get in touch with her natural gifts as a writer. And it also helped our son, Chip, discover his talents in business and leadership. By hearing—and occasionally seeing—their father doing the things he did during his career, they each had the opportunity to explore their own gifts and identify their unique calling.

It is also important to note that it was vital to our family for Dick to fulfill his role as provider (earning income). That's why Martha was supportive of him and understanding of his often-demanding travel schedule and was able to keep the home running smoothly while Dick was away.

But perhaps the most important lesson learned is one we all should remind ourselves of daily. Our unique calling or purpose is three-dimensional. In addition to what we do outside of the family, it also includes responsibly and faithfully fulfilling our roles within our families.

The Three Components of Our Natural Gifts

Our natural gifts can also be divided into three categories. The first category includes those gifts that are inherent—our *aptitudes*. For example, some people are more musically inclined than others, while other people may be more inclined to make or build things. But just because I have an aptitude for something doesn't necessarily mean I have the skills to respond to that aptitude. Being musically inclined, for example, doesn't make me a piano player. If I want to play the piano, I still must develop that ability.

These developed abilities we call *skills*. Skills are separate from aptitudes. We all know people who play various instruments skillfully, but because they lacked the aptitude, they aren't very good. Likewise, we probably know someone with great aptitude who is frustrated because they lack the skill to breathe life into that aptitude. This, then, leads us to the third component of our gifts: *motivation*.

In order to develop our gifts to our fullest potential, we must want to do so. If we don't want to, no matter how hard someone else pushes, no matter how challenging the circumstances we face, we simply won't reach our fullest potential.

Like the previous three-component diagrams, the more the circles overlap, the more fully developed your gifts will become as shown in figure 12.5. People who typically perform at the genius level in any domain (art, music, sports, writing, business, or technology, for example) have almost completely overlapping circles.

The Three Types of Supernatural Grace

The third component of this human trinity is God's supernatural grace. We cannot achieve human perfection without God, because as humans we are imperfect. Only God's grace can make up the difference between our imperfections and perfection.

There are three components to God's grace. These are: (1) *sanctifying*

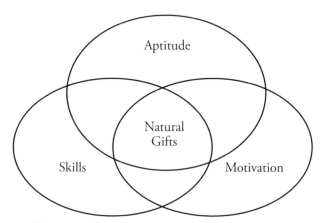

Figure 12.5 The Elements of Our Natural Gifts

grace, which is defined as "a stable and supernatural disposition that perfects the soul itself to enable it to live with God, to act by his love;" (2) *sacramental graces,* "which are gifts proper to the different sacraments," and (3) *special graces*, which are "also called *charisms*, after the Greek term used by St. Paul meaning "favor," "gratuitous gift," or "benefit."[17] These can also be depicted as overlapping circles to represent the fullness of God's graces as shown in figure 12.6. Sanctifying, or deifying, grace is the source of the work of sanctification. It is further comprised of both habitual grace and actual graces. *Habitual grace* is "the permanent disposition to live and act in keeping with God's call." *Actual graces* are "God's interventions," either "at the beginning of a conversion or in the course of the work of sanctification."[18]

Sacramental graces—gifts proper to the different sacraments—are the gifts many of us think about and associate ourselves with most often. For example, most Catholics get closer to God on a regular basis through reconciliation and Holy Communion.

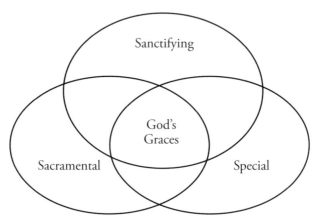

Figure 12.6 The Elements of Supernatural Grace

Some people benefit from *special graces* or charisms. Sometimes these charisms are extraordinary, "such as the gift of miracles or the gift of tongues." But whatever their character, special graces are intended "for the common good of the Church."[19]

Sometimes people refer to the *graces of state*—those graces "that accompany the exercise of responsibilities of the Christian life"—as a fourth category of graces. However, the *Catechism of the Catholic Church* places this grace in the category of special graces, thereby leaving us just three categories of grace.[20]

In summary then, our lives have three major components (purpose, gifts, graces) that are each further divided into three subcomponents, giving us nine elements to deal with effectively in order to achieve sanctity and answer God's call for us as individuals.

Our final and perhaps most important point regarding this framework for answering our call pertains to the question, "Why?"

Why Strive for Magnificence?

The answer: to achieve eternal happiness in God's kingdom. You may recall the teachings of the *Baltimore Catechism* about the purpose of our life: "to know, to love, and to serve God in this world and be happy with him forever in the next."[21] It sounds simple until you ask what it means *for you as an individual* to "serve God in this life." The only reasonable way to answer this question personally is to follow the example of the saints. One trait they all have in common is that they were able to combine their own natural gifts with God's supernatural grace to achieve a personal and unique purpose during their lives.

The following chapters explain how to identify your natural gifts and surround them with God's grace in order to fulfill your unique call.

***

I have set before you life and death, blessing and curse; therefore choose life, that you and your descendants may live, loving the LORD your God, obeying his voice, and clinging to him; for that means life to you and length of days, that you may dwell in the land which the LORD swore to your fathers, to Abraham, to Isaac, and to Jacob, to give them.

—Deuteronomy 30:19–20

CHAPTER THIRTEEN

Embrace Your Natural Gifts

Wouldn't it be nice if you were born with an operating manual that outlined all your gifts, explained exactly how to use them, showed how to troubleshoot when things weren't going right, and described in detail your life's purpose and your operating parameters as a human being?

However, in his divine wisdom, God gave us each a free will. If you had come complete with operating instructions, you would be deprived of your free will. This means it's up to you to discover your natural gifts and decide how best to combine them with God's grace so you can achieve your unique purpose in life and thereby answer your call. Consider the words of St. Paul:

> There are different kinds of spiritual gifts but the same Spirit; there are different forms of service but the same Lord; there are different workings but the same God who produces all of them in everyone. To each individual the manifestation of the Spirit is given for some benefit. (1 Corinthians 12:4–7, *NAB*)

Discovering Your Gifts

We all possess three kinds of natural gifts:

1. Those that are obvious early on and tend to develop naturally, which we call inherent gifts. For instance, an artist picks up a pencil at age four and renders a lifelike image.

2. Those that aren't obvious but develop in response to circumstance. These include gifts that may remain hidden until late in life. (Blessed Junipero Serra, for example, didn't realize his political gifts until he was in his sixties and in the middle of founding the California missions, when he had to use them to save the expedition.) Usually we refer to developed gifts as skills.

3. Motivation or passion for doing something or performing skills—either inherited or developed. For instance, a kindergartener loves to play catch, which Dad happily obliges.

As you work to discern your gifts, realize that those you identify today may not be those you ultimately use to serve God to your fullest potential. The best you can do is to work with what you have today, what you know today, and what your life's experiences teach you. Discernment of your gifts is a lifelong process. All you can hope for today is to get an answer based on what you know now.

Many people have a confused perception of their gifts because they try to view those gifts through the eyes of other people, either through what they've read or heard about others or through things others have said rather than through the correct interpretation of their own experiences. *Learning by experience can be a valuable teacher, but only if you learn the right lessons!* Here's how to learn the right lessons from your personal experiences to help you understand your unique gift mix.

Conduct a Personal Experience Audit

Make a list of seven times in your life when you were involved in making something meaningful happen. These should be experiences that describe situations where you made a difference and the outcome would have been different if you had not been involved.

Don't worry about being humble or focusing too much on yourself. You don't have to share the list with anyone unless you choose to do so. Here are recent lists we made—not good or bad, nor intended to set any sort of standard, but simply to serve as examples.

Martha's List:

1. Chairperson for Belle Benchley Elementary School Country Fair
2. Produced Eve Selis concert for a charitable cause
3. Organized, produced, and directed the Brownie troop play
4. Completed a seven-year Bible study course
5. Christmas on Quail Mountain
6. Easter on Quail Mountain
7. Dick's fortieth birthday party celebration
8. Organized First Sacraments program for St. Gabriel's parish

Dick's List:

1. Worked as a counselor at Boy Scout camp
2. Rescued a sailor from a lifeboat after his ship had sunk during a typhoon
3. Wrote a book about interpersonal effectiveness
4. Organized a celebrity charity golf tournament for Gene Tenace
5. Created a radio program called *The Catholic Business Hour*
6. Helped create a leadership training program for priests
7. Created a training program about management problem solving and decision making

The activities you mention on your list can be recent or something that happened years ago. They can be about big events or small. Whatever events you choose, however, should be events that gave you a sense of satisfaction, fulfillment, and a feeling of confidence that you made a positive difference.

Once you have created your list, write a four-part paragraph for each activity. The four parts of each paragraph should identify:

1. What you were trying to accomplish
2. The challenges you faced
3. How you overcame those challenges
4. The results you achieved

Martha might write a paragraph like the following for the second item on her list, "Produced an Eve Selis concert for a charitable cause."

> (1) The goal was to raise at least $15,000 for the bell tower at our church in a fun and entertaining way that involved the whole community of Poway. (2) The challenge was that not everyone in Poway is Catholic so non-Catholics might not want to participate, meaning we would raise less money. (3) I overcame the challenge, with the help of many others, by enlisting Eve Selis to perform and getting publicity in all the local newspapers and local TV stations. I asked our pastor to spread the word from the pulpit and to ask other pastors to do the same. I asked some of our local politicians to attend and recruited the mayor to be the master of ceremonies. I also arranged for food and beverages for people attending the concert and arranged to raffle off a guitar to the attendees. (4) The outcome was that everyone had a great time, the community got involved, we filled the auditorium, and we raised more than $35,000.

Martha is quick to point out that the concert was successful because of the efforts of many others (including Eve's mother and the family of Jessica Romag, in whose memory the concert was dedicated), and that she put her faith in God and let his will be done.

Dick wrote the following paragraph about the fifth item on his list, "Created a radio program called *The Catholic Business Hour*":

> (1) The goal was to create a radio program that would help a large number of Catholics find more meaning and rewards from their careers. (2) The challenges were that no one had ever offered a program like this, and I had never hosted a radio program. (3) I overcame those challenges by submitting a written proposal to a Catholic radio network that explained the need for such a program, how I thought it might be formatted, and when it should be aired. (4) The outcome was that the network responded favorably to the proposal, refined the idea, set up a studio in my home office in Poway, California, and launched the show, which now reaches hundreds of thousands of people.

Without comparing one paragraph to the next, write paragraphs like these for each of the seven items you've listed.

Once you've completed *all* seven paragraphs, reflect on them and look for patterns that exist between two or more. What are the strategies you used more than once? If you had to identify several skills, competencies, or talents that you used often, what would they be? Of all the skills, competencies, or talents you used more than once, which ones are your favorites? Which ones did you really enjoy using? Which ones didn't you like? Are there skills you feel more passionately about than others? Do they have anything in common? For example, are they skills that involve people, things, ideas, communication, art, or making things? If there were a big bucket in which you could put all your favorite skills, what would you name that bucket?

After studying the paragraphs for a while with these questions in mind, put them away for a day or two. Then come back and evaluate the paragraphs again. Repeat this process until you're ready to complete the following:

If I could group all my favorite skills, competencies, and talents into one or two skill buckets, this is what I would label as the most important:

1. _____

2. _____

Buckets are simply categories or groupings of different things you do well or like to do. For example, some people might list "working with people" as a bucket. Someone else might list "organizing projects and making them happen." Possible labels for buckets are almost endless. A few more labels for buckets might be: communicating with people, leading others, solving problems, building things, working with technology, coaching, writing, performing, and managing. Rather than finding a label for a bucket and trying to fit your gifts in that bucket, look at your gifts and see what buckets naturally emerge. Let your paragraphs reveal your buckets rather than choosing a bucket that you like and trying to make your gifts fit that bucket.

After studying her list, Martha concluded that her two favorite skill buckets should be labeled:

1. Organizing special events
2. Working with others

Dick's two favorite skill buckets from his list became:

1. Serving others
2. Communicating

Within each bucket, identify the top few skills, competencies, and talents—in other words, your natural gifts—that you tend to use when trying to accomplish things. List those gifts below each bucket:

Skill Bucket #1: _____

A. _____

B. _____

C. _____

D. _____

E. _____

Skill Bucket #2: _____

A. _____

B. _____

C. _____

D. _____

E. _____

After some reflection and discussion with others, Martha concluded that the skills she most tends to use in each of her two buckets are as follows:

Skill Bucket #1: Organizing Special Events

A. Planning

B. Organizing

C. Budgeting

D. Negotiating

E. Managing meetings

Skill Bucket #2: Working with Others

A. Recruiting volunteers

B. Delegating

C. Supervising

D. Motivating

E. Leading teams

Likewise, after some thought, Dick listed the following skills for his two buckets:

Skill Bucket #1: Serving Others
A. Coaching
B. Consulting
C. Problem solving
D. Training
E. Giving feedback

Skill Bucket #2: Communicating
A. Public speaking
B. Writing
C. Giving clear direction
D. Listening
E. Receiving feedback

There are no right or wrong answers, nor is there one best set of natural gifts. These examples are merely meant to provide ideas about what your gift mix might look like. If you'd like additional perspectives on looking at different skill sets and how they relate to different career choices, you might consider browsing the Internet.

There are numerous resources on the Internet, some that are free and don't require any registration, some that require registration, and others that require fees. All you need do is Google "personal skill assessment." Yahoo!Hotjobs, for example, has different kinds of job search-related assessments that are free but require you to register. Unless you are truly stymied in your quest for personal understanding, we recommend staying away from those that charge a fee. It's unlikely you'll gain much more insight than you will by completing the exercises we've outlined in this chapter and augmenting them with a few of the free assessments you'll find online.

It's also worth noting that your quest to understand your natural gifts should be seen as a lifelong process, not a one-time event. History is replete with tales of people whose greatest natural gifts didn't emerge until later in life, in situations or circumstances they never would have predicted earlier in life (such as St. Augustine). One of life's greatest wonders is that we all have hidden gifts and talent germinating beneath the surface, waiting for the right circumstance to blossom forth in a way that brings glory and honor to God, and touching the world and other people in a positive way.

> "These differences belong to God's plan, who wills that each receive what he needs from others, and that those endowed with particular 'talents' share the benefits with those who need them. These differences encourage and often oblige persons to practice generosity, kindness, and sharing of goods; they foster the mutual enrichment of cultures."
>
> —*CCC*, 1937

CHAPTER FOURTEEN

Understanding Discernment in Relation to Purpose and Call

The Church tackles all the big questions, like the purpose of life: "to know, to love, and to serve God in this life and to be happy with him forever in the next."[22] However, because God gave us each a free will, the Church leaves it up to each one of us to determine the meaning of *service* for ourselves. What does "to serve God in this life" mean for you? Your answer should have several facets.

Your Calling Is Three-Dimensional

Many Catholic theologians throughout history have taught that each of us has a unique purpose, a unique mission, in life. Your individual purpose relates to your natural gifts, and it's up to you to combine with God's supernatural grace to achieve sanctity.

Your purpose in life extends far beyond your job title. Work—defined as both the paid and unpaid energy we expend to make the world a better place— is only one dimension of your purpose. You also have a faith dimension and a family dimension. You have potential for fulfillment in each of these three areas, but they are not separate from one another. You can only fulfill your purpose—and answer your call—if you fulfill them *together.* How many people go through life without realizing this? What a shame!

Putting Discernment in Perspective

Seminars focused on personal empowerment enjoy great popularity today. Lasting anywhere from a couple hours to several days, one of their common characteristics is that most include an exercise where the participants develop a "life purpose statement" or a "life mission statement." These experiences are motivating for the moment and cause people to leave the group with a feeling of euphoria and a sense that they "have figured their life out" or "really know who they are." Unfortunately, though, most just end up kidding themselves about the value of what they've done. It's like driving your car through a robo-wash and expecting it to glisten for years. Wouldn't it be nice if determining your calling were that easy? Unfortunately, it is not.

Discernment takes effort. It also takes time. Discerning how to best answer your call is a lifelong process. Throughout our lives we face decisions regarding family, career, marriage, education (either for us or our families), housing, health, lifestyle, and hundreds of other important issues. Each of these decisions should be made in communion with God— through prayer, meditation, and reflection. You speak to God through your prayers *and* through your actions.

He then responds to you by speaking to you in a number of different ways. In reviewing the various ways he can speak to you, it is important to remember that although God is perfect and infallible, *you are not*. This means that sometimes you won't get the message right. Both history and our modern world are rife with examples of people who somehow came to believe they were getting messages from God when they were not.

This is one reason why we call it a process of discernment rather than decision-making. Discernment implies an ongoing process of discrimination and refinement in judgment that relies on multiple sources of input and objective evaluation, whereas decision-making means choosing one choice among a finite set of alternatives. It may help to consider the meaning of the word *discern*: to distinguish, to separate by sifting. It is a dynamic process that involves the passage of time and careful consideration. By definition, discernment cannot happen in a flash—despite what we see in the movies, where decision-making appears to be a split-second act as planes are boarding and brides are walking down the aisle.

Let's consider an example here to make the point. A businessman who is trying to decide whether to expand into a new territory thinks it's a good idea and pretty much concludes that is what he wants to do. He attends morning Mass and stays afterward to pray about his decision. He says a few prayers, during which he might even ask for God's guidance. Then he asks himself if it is still a good idea. He concludes it is still a good idea, so he goes ahead with the decision, assured in his own mind he has prayerfully discerned the decision. Wrong! He hasn't discerned anything. He has prayed, and he has decided. But he hasn't *discerned* because he hasn't given God a chance to communicate! The process of discernment must allow time for God to communicate or it's not a process of discernment at all.

How Does God Communicate to Us?

The mere idea of listening to God communicate scares many people. "I'm not Moses!" they might say, or "I'm no prophet," or "I'm not worthy of God speaking to me." They may worry that the message they hear has come from the occult. Others lack patience or fear hearing something contrary to their own personal preference, so they just stay quiet and ignore the topic altogether. The fact is, however, that God communicates to all of us in various ways, and we can all benefit by listening more closely and more openly.

God speaks to us through the Gospels. God anticipated our needs through the passages of Scripture. It is important to read and study the Bible on an ongoing basis, because different passages will take on differing degrees of relevance at different times in your life. You may have read something a year ago and not thought too much about it at the time because of your circumstances at the time. Today, however, you might be dealing with a different set of concerns and that same passage might take on a completely different meaning and carry with it a completely different sense of importance. You'll never cease to be startled by new ways Scripture can speak to you. "Late it was that I loved you, beauty so ancient and so new," St. Augustine proclaimed.[23] Indeed, the ancient words of Scripture are ever new. The slant of the sun and of our hearts never repeats itself two days in a row. What sounded easy yesterday feels difficult today. What challenged us last time comforts us this time around.

God speaks to us through the teachings of the Catholic Church, our priests, bishops, and other religious, including spiritual directors. A practice that had fallen out of favor, but fortunately seems to be rebounding today, is the habit of having a spiritual director. Everyone who is serious about integrating their faith with the other dimensions of their life should consider having a spiritual director. This is a person who is an authentic Catholic (preferably a priest or deacon), grounded in the teachings of the Church, and can help apply those teachings to everyday life. The Church's teachings are based on the truth and have been refined through the creation of a comprehensive *Catechism* and thousands of other documents, including papal encyclicals and books. No other religion in the world benefits from as much study, analysis, and clarification of Jesus's teachings as the Catholic Church. So listen to your priests and bishops. Listen to discern what God has to say to you about how you should be living your life.

Converts often help us cradle Catholics appreciate the richness of our faith. Jennifer Fulwiler, a thirty-something Texas blogger, expressed it well in a *National Catholic Register* blog post:

"...within the two-thousand-year-old Church is an unfathomable treasure chest of spiritual wisdom. We have the Rosary as well as all the other time-tested prayers of the Church. Then there are the lives of the saints, countless stories that offer an inexhaustible supply of information and inspiration about how to have a rich spiritual life. And of course we have a worldwide network of monasteries and convents, and all the great religious orders. I suppose it's possible to utilize some of these spiritual resources without being a practicing Catholic, but if you believe that they're good and helpful, why sever them from the source of their wisdom?"[24]

God speaks to us through circumstances. These messages are often the most clear. For example, when someone loses her job—regardless of the reason—the message is clear: that's probably not where God wanted that person to be at that time. Perhaps he has a better plan. Circumstances change. Examples abound of people who were called to be in one situation, then over time the situation changed and they were called to another. In the words of St. Nilus Sorsky: "Nothing that happens to us is contrary to the will of Providence, and everything that is sent us by God is for our good and the salvation of our soul. Even if it does not seem beneficial at the present moment, we shall understand later that it is what is willed by God, and not what we desire that is useful to us."[25] Experience can be a valuable teacher, but only if we learn the right lessons from them. This is one reason why it is so important to remember that discernment is an ongoing, never-ending process.

God speaks to us through visions and dreams. Consider Acts 22:17: "When I had returned to Jerusalem and was praying in the temple, I fell into a trance...." Another biblical example comes from the Apostle Paul in subsequent verses of Acts. His plan to serve God was to stay in Jerusalem and preach to those who knew him. Then, during a vision, God revealed that God's plan for his life was different. "...and [I] saw him saying to me, 'Make haste and get quickly out of Jerusalem, because they will not accept your testimony about me'" (Acts 22:18).

God speaks to us through the grace of peace. If you are surrounded by peace, it is likely you are doing God's will. When there is no peace, it is equally as likely that you are outside of God's will, although sometimes you might be doing God's will and still not experience peace. It's necessary to exercise discernment. If you are not experiencing peace, is it because you're outside God's will? Possibly. But you can experience peace even in tumultuous circumstances.

God speaks to us through likenesses or images so powerful that they make a profound imprint on our minds. One name for these powerful images is "similitude." Hosea 12:10 says, "I spoke to the prophets; / it was I who multiplied visions, / and through the prophets gave parables." Human beings are by nature drawn to images of themselves they see projected into the future. The more vivid and powerful these images are, the more we will be drawn to them. If you can't see yourself projected in a certain manner into the future, chances are you are not being called in that direction. Can you picture this person as your spouse? Can you see yourself enjoying this job? If you are confronted with powerful images, maybe even so strong that you can't get them out of your mind, then this could very well be God speaking to you.

God speaks to us directly. Sometimes he does this out loud, with an audible voice as he did with Moses. Other times he does so inaudibly but nonetheless directly. Most often this happens during prayer. It's important to always open your prayers with the sign of the cross or to pray in Jesus's name to ensure that it is Jesus you hear. But in order for this to happen during prayer, guess what? We must be listening! Consider the words of the theologian William Barclay:

It may be that one of our great faults in prayer is that we talk too much and listen too little. When prayer is at its highest we wait in silence for God's voice to us; we linger in His presence for His peace and His power to flow over us and around us; we lean back in His everlasting arms and feel the serenity of perfect security in Him.[26]

It should be easy for us to pray; we have plenty of opportunities. In addition to praying often, Catholics should also receive the Eucharist as often as possible. Most of us are fortunate to have the opportunity to participate in the Eucharist daily. It's up to each of us to avoid the busyness and tune out the noise that gives us a perceived reason to flee from a vibrant interior life. Take heart in the following words from Pope Benedict XVI:

...for in sacramental communion I become one with the Lord, like all the other communicants. As Saint Paul says, "Because there is one bread, we who are many are one body, for we all partake of the one bread" (1 Cor. 10:17). Union with Christ is also union with all those to whom he gives himself. I cannot possess Christ just for myself; I can belong to him only in union with all those who have become, or who will become, his own. Communion draws me out of myself towards him, and thus also towards unity with all Christians. We become "one body," completely joined in a single existence. Love of God and love of neighbor are now truly united: God incarnate draws us all to himself.[27]

Of course, we each have days when we desperately need to be drawn out of ourselves—toward community, toward God, toward a higher ground. The Eucharist nurtures us in our quest to become closer to God, to others, and to our calling. It is this closeness to others that leads us to yet another way God can speak to us.

God speaks to us through other people. We all make up the body of Christ, with Jesus as the head. Sometimes Jesus speaks to us through others. Occasionally this happens through the gift of prophecy. Other times it happens very simply, by way of the things people say to us, either as feedback or in response to questions we might ask. This doesn't mean we should let others rule our lives. Nor does it mean everyone else is always right about what's right for us. Earlier, in Chapters 8 and 9, we showed how other people can often steer us in the wrong direction, either in regard to our calling or our gifts. Peer pressure does not always push us in the right direction. So it is important that we are extremely careful in discerning input from others. But we should never ignore it.

Mitch Albom, author of *Tuesdays With Morrie*, the top-selling memoir in publishing history, was profoundly changed by the words his beloved professor Morrie offered up in his dying months. Mitch addressed this reality in an interview with CatholicMatch, saying:

> We're in a world where computers and media and the Internet are dominating our lives, and we're looking for places halfway around the world to connect with people and celebrities we're never going to meet...we're listening to their tweets of 140 characters, holding them up as some kind of dogma. In my mind, the greatest wisdom you're ever going to find is probably going to be about a mile from your house—someone you know or were raised with from your church or synagogue who is going to speak to you and know your life.[28]

In his first encyclical, *Deus Caritas Est* (God Is Love), Pope Benedict XVI cautions against hardheartedness. We need to open ourselves to others, he writes, to be softened and stretched: "Love of neighbor is a path that leads to the encounter with God, and that closing our eyes to our neighbor also blinds us to God." The Holy Father continues:

… if in my life I fail completely to heed others, solely out of a desire to be "devout" and to perform my "religious duties," then my relationship with God will also grow arid. It becomes merely "proper," but loveless. Only my readiness to encounter my neighbour and to show him love makes me sensitive to God as well. Only if I serve my neighbour can my eyes be opened to what God does for me and how much he loves me. The saints—consider the example of Blessed Teresa of Calcutta— constantly renewed their capacity for love of neighbour from their encounter with the Eucharistic Lord, and conversely this encounter acquired its realism and depth in their service to others. Love of God and love of neighbor are thus inseparable, they form a single commandment. But both live from the love of God who has loved us first. No longer is it a question, then, of a "commandment" imposed from without and calling for the impossible, but rather a freely-bestowed experience of love from within, a love which by its very nature must then be shared with others.[29]

What a blessing—and what a relief—that God speaks to us in multiple ways, for we each hear differently. Sometimes we pick it up clearly, and sometimes we don't get it right at all. Discernment is an ongoing, never-ending process that we should embrace as a key element of our lifestyle, along with prayer and the Eucharist.

Four Criteria for Determining Your Calling

1. *Your calling should be three-dimensional, addressing faith, family, and work (things we do, both paid and unpaid, that make the world a better place).*

For Catholics, the faith dimension is straightforward: We should all strive to be *authentic Catholics*. According to Archbishop Charles Chaput: "The authentic Catholic layperson in the 21st century is a person who really believes in Jesus and really believes what the Church teaches—about sin, suffering, the Cross, the physical Resurrection, heaven, hell, the reality of the supernatural, our vocation to transform this world and care for it, the dignity of every person and a commitment to the common good through social justice and care for the poor."[30]

This is easy to say but hard to do in this day and age. Archbishop Chaput recognized this, and he put it in no uncertain terms: "We need to love the world, but we also need to shed any illusions about the compatibility of the spirit of our age and the spirit of Jesus. *They are enemies.*"[31]

The family dimension is also straightforward for Catholics, but we often forget that it is multidimensional. We have responsibilities to the family we were born into as well as the family we create, which can require a lot of us. Without question, the best role model for family is the Holy Family. Seek the Holy Family's wisdom and their prayerful intercession.

The work dimension, for a variety of reasons, is often the most challenging, because we tend to see it as separate from both the faith and family dimensions. Even worse, we might see it as something that *interferes* with faith and family. We know of one young man who graduated from college and received two job offers. One would initially require working more than forty hours per week, the other only forty. The first job would also require taking some work home from time to time to complete during the evenings or over the weekend, whereas the second job was self-contained during those base forty hours. But the first job also paid more. The young man took the less demanding job that paid less because he wanted to spend more time with his wife and two young kids. While this sounds very family focused, a problem arose when they didn't have enough money to pay all the bills. The wife had to take a three-quarter-time job to help make ends meet. On top of that, much of the husband's time on the weekends was not spent with family. He was playing golf, camping, fishing with friends, and so on. At this stage of their lives, did the young man make the best decision for his family? Working harder to provide more income and stability and then spending *quality* time rather than *more* time with the family, would have been a much better decision at this time in his life.

Today young couples get caught in the two-income trap. They marry, they both work, and they become accustomed to their two-income lifestyle and all it affords: the most expensive cable package, the newest version of the iPad, vacations, concerts. Their cost-cutting neighbors who are parents knowingly dub them DINKs: Dual Income, No Kids. When these young couples decide to have a family, they don't feel that they can afford to give up their dual income. They find themselves caught between having a family and having two incomes. Many decide to keep their full-time jobs *and* start a family. But more often than not, frustration and resentment creep in, even if they like the work they're doing. The husband grows resentful of his job because it doesn't pay enough to support his family at the level to which they've become accustomed. The wife becomes frustrated because her job takes her away from her family, and she now is trying to balance two full-time careers—that of homemaker and mother with her other job. She may not have anticipated just how strong a pull she feels to her children. This frustration and resentment drain energy from a vibrant faith life, putting a strain on the family while detracting from on-the-job work performance. This in turn leads to fewer pay raises, slower advancement, and even greater career frustration. Everyone suffers.

The way to avoid this frustration is to recognize from the outset that faith, family, and work are all important—and that to honor this importance we should choose both a lifestyle and an approach toward life that allow us to perform well in all dimensions *given our current circumstances.*

2. Your calling should be characterized by a personal passion strong enough to endure the tests of time and hardship.

Men who are called to the priesthood have an advantage because their formation in the seminary takes so long. After six to nine years in the seminary, most can rest assured that their passion will carry them through the challenges they will face in the future.

The reason we get engaged prior to marrying is so we can test our passion for our potential spouses and our ability to endure a lifetime of challenges with each other. We should have the same attitude about our work. Do I have the passion to strive for magnificence in all I do throughout the ups and downs of an entire career? If not, what work should I be doing that will afford me this passion? Don't look for an *employer* who will motivate you. Look for *work* that ignites your zeal. If you genuinely look forward to the work you do, gain satisfaction and fulfillment from its accomplishment, and feel as though it is work you are suited to perform, then all the extrinsic rewards—such as pay, advancement, and benefits— will come to you. Too many people look for a good *job*—one that pays well, has a reasonable commute, and good hours. Not enough people look for good work: work that is satisfying, enjoyable, and intrinsically rewarding.

3. *You should be able to put your calling ahead of self in all three dimensions (faith, family, and work).*

Remember the *Catechism*: The purpose of our life is "to know, to love, and to serve God in this life and to be happy with Him forever in the next." Realize that what is *not* said here should be taken into account as well. The *Catechism* does not say that our goal in life should be to accumulate wealth, strive for fame and celebrity, or pursue self-serving, materialistic goals. This is not to say that either wealth or celebrity status is bad. History is replete with examples of people who have used their accumulated wealth, fame, or power to achieve great good. But it does mean that any earthly trappings of success should be the means to an end of service to God and fellow man, not an end in itself. It takes great humility to maintain this perspective, which is why humility is a requirement for valid discernment, which leads us to the next criterion.

4. *Your calling should enable you to look beyond what you think you might be capable of today to what you believe you might be able to do when your full potential is developed.*

Remember when Moses said, "But I'm not the right person for this job," even as God made his request directly to Moses? And what was God's reply? He told Moses that he wouldn't ask him to do something without being there to help him. In other words, if you can do it without God's help, it's probably not a very ambitious calling. Your calling must be lofty enough that it can't be fulfilled without God's grace. Your call relies on your natural gifts, combined with God's grace, to achieve your unique purpose. If you can achieve what you've set out for yourself without God's grace, you are not answering your full and true call.

Mistakes Along the Way

Once a woman called Dick's radio show and asked for advice on whether or not she should start a new business. In this case, it was a Catholic bookstore. The thought had occurred to her two weeks earlier when she developed a feeling she was being called in this direction. This was the week before Lent. She wanted to decide quickly because, if this was the right decision for her, she wanted to open her doors right after Easter. Everyone she talked to, mostly people in her parish, thought it was a great idea and encouraged her to jump right on it. Then she called the radio show.

Dick asked her who in the Catholic bookstore industry she had talked to about her idea. The answer was no one. He asked her how many other Catholic bookstores were in her community. She said there was only one, and it was struggling. Dick asked her how many bookstores of any kind were in her community and how they were doing. She didn't know. Dick asked her if she or her husband had any experience in retail store operations, and she said they had none. He asked if either of them had any experience in owning or operating a small business, and her answer was again negative. Do you get the picture?

This woman was getting ready to make a serious decision without any of the most basic information required. Without this information, she was bound to make a bad decision. Of course, bad decisions might turn out well due to circumstances beyond our control, but the reverse is also true. Sometimes good decisions turn out badly due to circumstances beyond our control. But at every point in our lives, it is important that we make the best decisions possible, using the best information available in order to give ourselves the highest probability of success.

Dick advised her to take her time with the decision. He encouraged her to talk to other people in the same business, as well as other businesspeople and bankers. He suggested she might even take a job working in a bookstore for a while to find out what it would be like to be there fifty hours a week. He also suggested she look at the local market situation.

Could her community support another Catholic bookstore? In summary, he gave her a list of questions to answer and some fairly extensive research to conduct. Only after answering all the questions and conducting all the research would it be wise to consider such a serious decision. He said she should spend at least six months thoroughly investigating the idea and then, if she decided to pursue it, she possibly could be open by Lent of the *following* year.

As you discern God's call for you, you should follow a similar thought and discernment process. If you can figure it out in a week or two, God bless you and Godspeed. Most people can't, even though they think they can in this world of instant gratification, which is why so many people are unsatisfied.

You can't get it right by simply relying on tests, either. Remember taking those vocational aptitude tests in school—the ones that asked for a series of preferences and then compared your preference profile to people working in various fields? If you do, then you might also remember them telling you what career you might be suited for. However, many of these tests fail to take into account that anywhere between 75 and 85 percent of the working population are dissatisfied with their careers—which means that if your profile matches those in a certain career, you also have a 75 to 85 percent chance of being just as dissatisfied if you choose that career.

In summary, avoid rushing into decisions. Gather information and input from a variety of sources, but don't view any one source as the source that will give you a quick and easy answer. Discernment takes time and effort.

An Approach for Discerning Your Purpose

There is no "best" way to discern purpose that will work perfectly for everyone. Therefore, it's your responsibility to discover what works best for you. However, the following outline presents key elements of a four-phase process that will provide a solid foundation for your approach.

The first phase is *data gathering*. During this phase you'll gather as much information from as many *valid* sources as possible for you to use in your discernment process. The second phase is *analysis and evaluation*. Here you evaluate and interpret the information you've gathered in light of your current circumstances. During the third phase, *clarification*, you define your purpose. This is where you make personal commitments based on your Phase 2 assessment. During the fourth phase, *implementation*, you begin to live your calling as you've come to understand it while you continue to discern. *If you are married, we suggest you and your spouse complete all four phases of the discernment process together.* (Phases 1 and 2 are joint activities, while Phases 3 and 4 are more individually focused.)

Before launching into the process, determine a rough time frame for completing each phase that will be realistic for you, given your current life situation. For example, a high-school student might use freshman and sophomore years to gather information, followed by junior year for analysis and evaluation. This would set the student up to be able to start living his or her call by applying to the right colleges and preparing for graduation during senior year.

Someone in mid-career might set aside anywhere from one to six months for data gathering, another few months for evaluating and interpreting the information, a month or more to reach the new commitments, and then some kind of transition time to move from their current situation to the newly chosen path. The whole process might take anywhere from a few months to a year.

An individual approaching retirement might take years to complete all the steps. Knowing when retirement is likely to occur, he or she may start the process two, three, five, or even ten years ahead of time. Part of the assessment process might be volunteering or working part-time in certain arenas to actually test whether or not that setting is appropriate for a longer-term decision. That's one useful way, among others, to gather information.

Given your current situation, what kind of time frame do you need to complete each phase? Write your answer now on a sheet of paper. You'll revisit this time frame after you've learned more about what each phase should accomplish. Now let's examine each phase in more detail.

Phase 1: Data Gathering

Your goal during Phase 1 is to gather as much information as possible about yourself that will allow you to clarify God's calling for you at this time in your life. Valid and reliable information drives good decisions. Information regarding you and your calling comes from several sources. It is important that you glean whatever information is possible from as many of these sources as you can in order to provide the best input for your decisions. Arrange the information in a manner that will allow you to store it and retrieve it in the future. Later in life, as you go through subsequent discernment processes, it will be helpful to be able to refer back to this information and refresh your memory about those issues that have guided your discernment process.

One way to organize the information is in a three-ring binder, creating different tabbed sections with appropriate titles. Another way to organize the material—which we highly recommend—is using an expandable, accordion-type file folder with multiple pockets. These come in all sizes, but one of the most common is constructed with a pocket for each letter of the alphabet. This might work well if you are going to include information like printed test results, printed profiles, or information in a format that might not be easy to put in a three-ring binder.

Once you've decided how you're going to organize the material, start collecting as much information as you can. The information will be derived from numerous sources. Here's a list of several you might use:

1. Your personal memory
2. The memories of people close to you (friends, family, colleagues, teachers, coworkers, mentors)
3. Aptitude tests (many of which are available at no or low cost on the Internet)
4. Articles that might have been written about you
5. Awards you've received
6. Recognition that came your way

The first step is to start compiling the information by generating three lists. The first list should be a list of all the things you can remember you ever really wanted to do with your life. Label this "Life Choices I've Considered." Go back in your life as far as you can remember. Include everything, regardless of how other people may have reacted to it, how young you were when you entertained it, or anything negative that might have developed in your own mind about a particular choice. In other words, don't say something like this to yourself: "All through elementary school I wanted more than anything to be a nurse, but my parents said I'd never be good at it, so I dropped the idea. Therefore, I won't put it on the list." For the time being, forget what others said. If you were attracted to something for whatever reason, list it.

You might even consider segmenting this list. The first part might be choices you considered in elementary school, the second part might be choices you considered in middle school, and the third might be choices you thought about in high school. If you went to college, include a section about college. You should also have a section that covers the post-schooling period. Depending on your age, you might also have an early career, mid-career, and late-career section.

The key here is to recall what you really wanted to be at different times in your life. Don't judge, evaluate, or assess at this point in time—merely capture and record. Compiling this list should take at least several days—and it might even take a few weeks. Once this list is in process, start on your second list.

Create a list of the activities you most enjoy doing. Label this list "Activities I Have Enjoyed." Think of the times in your life when you have truly enjoyed what you've been doing, and add them to the list. The enjoyment could have been sparked by various reasons, but don't worry about that now. Simply list the things you've done that have brought you joy on a level that is meaningful to you. Some examples people have included are:

- learned to play the piano
- taught swimming and lifesaving lessons for the American Red Cross
- coached Pop Warner football
- taught CCD classes for our parish
- wrote a short story
- ran in a triathlon
- volunteered at the local homeless shelter, worked as an administrative assistant
- made a quilt
- biked along a river
- went to the movies

Again, you might consider organizing the list according to different periods of time in your life. Do what's easiest for you. We've found that by segmenting the list, some people actually rediscover activities they thoroughly enjoyed that their life circumstances have since kept them from doing. For example, one man was actively involved in helping younger Boy Scouts while he was a high-school student. He went away to college, and his involvement ceased. Years later he realized how much he missed that involvement, found a local troop, and started volunteering again. The story has a happy ending, but think of all the years he missed.

Your third list will contain all the opportunities that came your way during your life that you *did not* take advantage of. Label this list "Opportunities I Did Not Pursue." This will be a shorter list than the other two, and it will probably be a bit harder to compile. It is nonetheless important, because these opportunities have come your way for a reason. The reason may not have been apparent to you at the time the opportunity presented itself, but it is important that you understand it now so you can discern properly going forward. For example, one woman was asked to teach CCD at her parish. "Why are they asking me?" she thought. "I've never taught before, and besides I'm busy with my own family right now." She declined. It turns out the reason she was asked was because all the other teachers recognized her love of the faith and the wonderful way she presented and talked about her beliefs. Years later, she was "pressed into service" during the middle of the school year when another teacher took ill. She reluctantly filled in. In no time at all she discovered that her natural gifts blossomed as a CCD teacher. Sometimes we need that push.

When an opportunity comes your way, it does so for a reason, even if you can't immediately see the reason yourself. Always remember that we are all one body with Christ as the head. Sometimes Jesus will speak to you through the actions of the rest of the body. When that happens, make sure you listen.

After you've started compiling these three lists, the next step in the information-gathering phase is to collect as much information about yourself as possible to begin filling the pockets in your accordion folder. Photocopy any awards you've received and file each in one of the slots. Do the same with any letter of commendation or other recognition you've received during your life. If you don't have the original document, simply jot down a note about it and include that in the file. Write down any compliments you've received from other people and put those pieces of paper in the appropriate folder. File away thank-you notes that express appreciation for a certain trait. You might struggle with this exercise, thinking it is too prideful or self-centered. But don't worry—you are going to look at this information objectively, with a discerning mind-set, not in a conceited or prideful way.

Next, gather all the vocational assessment information you can find about yourself. Get copies of old assessment reports. Take new assessments online (look for those that are free). File all this information in your folder without attempting to draw any conclusions. Let the information speak for itself. At this stage of the process, don't make the mistake of shooting from the hip and making snap judgments about what everything means. This almost always leads to poor discernment.

Again, allow yourself at least several days to complete the information gathering. If it takes several weeks, or even months, that's okay. Once you're absolutely convinced that you've been as thorough as possible and exhausted all possible sources of information, you can proceed to Phase 2.

Phase 2: Analysis and Interpretation

Your goal during Phase 2 is to examine all the information gathered in Phase 1 to determine what it means to you. Are there any patterns or consistencies you can identify? Are there items that you once thought were true and valid but have since found to be invalid?

Your biggest challenge here is to be objective. Avoid manipulating the data to validate foregone conclusions. Let yourself be surprised! Let the information challenge your assumptions about yourself, past choices, and the conclusions you may have already drawn. If you are married and completing this process with your spouse, this is a great time to challenge each other's past assumptions and help each other identify strengths and potential that each of you both may have neglected in yourself. We suggest that you include other people at this stage of the process as well. They should be people who can help you by adding objectivity, providing more information and insight, or facilitating your deliberations in some meaningful way. You might choose a close friend you consider a confidant, your spiritual director or pastor, a teacher or a mentor, a respected colleague, or people from different vocations or professions who might be able to add insight to your analysis.

When involving others, be careful to ensure that you get the feedback and input you need, rather than mere validation of what people think you want to hear. A mistake when asking for this kind of help is not asking those who will tell the absolute truth as they see it. This truth is often very different from what you might like to hear. Don't get input from people who will only validate your foregone conclusions. Don't steer them in a way that may influence their perception of what you seek. Tell those you choose that the feedback and input they provide will only be helpful if it is honest and accurate, regardless of whether or not it is desired.

There are three worksheets that will help during this phase of the process. If you and your spouse are doing this together, you'll probably want to do three worksheets for each of you and then repeat the exercise, completing three worksheets for you as a couple.

Label the first worksheet "Themes" and then cull through all the information you have compiled and search for recurring themes that emerge. For example, one person we worked with concluded that at every stage of her life people had approached her and said she should write more. Throughout her life people encouraged her to write short stories, novels, and even nonfiction books. The fact that she had always discounted these statements because she didn't consider herself to be a skilled writer didn't matter. Because this issue surfaced on numerous occasions, she was right to list this as a theme emerging from her data. Another person we know listed music as a theme, because almost everything he did that he enjoyed involved music. Yet another listed teaching as a theme because her most fulfilling activities always centered around teaching, training, coaching, or helping others to learn in some way. Here are few examples of the kinds of themes people often identify. These are only examples; there could be hundreds more.

Working with people	Working with wood
Building things	Leading people
Working in the church	Working with children
Being part of a group	Being more independent
Using my creativity	Relying on myself
Being entrepreneurial	Solving problems
Serving others	Selling

Once you've made a good effort to identify themes, label a second worksheet "Patterns." Sift back through all the information you've compiled to try to identify patterns of behavior or responses you've made in different situations to the input, feedback, and opportunities that came your way.

One man found that everything he became involved with ended up with his being asked to take a leadership role. This started when he played sports in high school and was the captain of two different teams. In college he became president of his fraternity. Later in his career he became the head of the local Chamber of Commerce, a leader in his local chapter of the Knights of Columbus, and head of the local Little League organization. It's safe to say in his case that during his life he clearly demonstrated a pattern of being drawn to leadership positions.

Patterns do not necessarily have to be lifelong. Some patterns emerge only during certain phases of our lives. Many parents, for example, find themselves drawn into volunteer roles they would not have considered prior to becoming parents. Volunteering in the girls' softball league, with the Brownie troop, and at school with the class play might all have come about only because you are a parent. But now that it has happened—and if it happens several times—it qualifies as a pattern and should be added to the list.

The third worksheet should be labeled "Things I've Missed." Here you look for something you may have overlooked before. Is there an unfulfilled interest that popped up more than once? Did you ever receive feedback from a close friend that made you recall or reconsider a goal? There may be one or two events that occurred in your life that weren't repeated often enough to be labeled either a theme or a pattern but might reveal something special about you. Maybe you were only in the right circumstance once or twice for a particular role to present itself, and if more such circumstances had arisen you might have shown that attribute more often. For example, maybe you were one of the first people to arrive at the scene of a bad accident. Of all the bystanders, you stepped up and directed traffic around the accident until the authorities arrived. This isn't the type of experience we have every day. But it's likely you would have been recognized and appreciated by others for taking charge of a negative situation and making it better.

Phase 3: Final Clarification and Commitment

Your goal during Phase 3 is to reach conclusions and gain clarity about your overall life's purpose. In light of everything you've done up to this point, now it is time to clarify your life's purpose. If you are doing this as a couple, you will each clarify your own personal purpose, and then you will also clarify your purpose as a couple.

In order to have wholeness and integration in your life, your final clarification of purpose should address each department of your life: faith, family, and work. You probably won't end up with some cleverly crafted phrase that will put everything in perspective. It's more likely that you'll end up with a few paragraphs about you, your spouse, and yourselves as a couple that address each of the three departments of your life.

The next three chapters take you through a process for discerning each of the three departments. Faith is addressed first, followed by family, and finally, work.

Phase 4: Living with Continued Discernment

Your goal during Phase 4 is to live your calling in a manner that brings glory and honor to God, having confidence that you are where God wants you to be today, yet realizing that things may change in the future.

How you live your calling is every bit as important as *what* you do in pursuit of your calling. Let's look at what happens by not realizing this. We know of a Catholic lay organization that has as its purpose to spread the Gospel in support of the New Evangelization. This as a noble cause, and many talented people are called to serve in this organization because they believe they have something to contribute. The founders and leaders of the organization, however, have been leadership-challenged from the beginning. The biggest issue is a complete lack of empathy. They mismanage people, treat employees with disrespect, and have created an arid, non-nurturing culture that is cold, driven by fear, and lacking in integrity. What a shame! They can't be successful in spreading the gospel if they don't first make a credible effort to live it themselves. Participating in Catholic ritual is meaningless unless that participation leads to behavior that reflects Christ's teachings. We must be authentic in our everyday actions.

If part of your calling is to have a positive impact on the world around you, then you must first and always maintain a strong commitment to be a valid personal example of this. This doesn't mean you must be perfect, but it does mean you strive to be congruent and authentic in all your actions. Chapter twenty goes into more detail about how to pursue your calling in a congruent way.

CHAPTER FIFTEEN

Discern Your Faith Purpose

To be able to determine what God wants you to do with your life, you must first answer a more basic question: "What does God want?" Once you answer that, you can then answer the question: "What does God want *from me?*"

Archbishop Chaput gave a great answer in a speech he delivered to priests in the Philadelphia Archdiocese in the fall of 2005. He said that God wants one thing: God wants to save the soul of the world in the name of his son, Jesus Christ.[32] That means each of us must accept the responsibility to *first* save our own soul, *and then* we must actively help save the souls of others.

Consider the words of John Paul II: "We are engaged in a struggle for the soul of the contemporary world."[33] If this is true, we need to recover the traditional Christian image of spiritual warfare. The *Catechism* states: "The whole of man's history has been the story of dour combat with the powers of evil, stretching, so our Lord tells us, from the very dawn of history until the last day. Finding himself in the midst of the battlefield man has to struggle to do what is right, and it is at great cost to himself, and aided by God's grace, that he succeeds in achieving his own inner integrity" (*CCC*, 409).[34]

Our weapons are not guns or hatred or religious prejudice—they are courage, honesty, charity, knowledge, clarity, excellence that leads to magnificence, and truth rooted in the person of Jesus Christ and rooted in the cross he carried for us. Therefore, it is up to each of us to determine how we are going to fulfill this call. People frequently ask us if they should quit their job and work for the Church so they can serve God more directly. Our answer is maybe—but probably not.

What role will you play in the struggle? God put you where you are for a reason. Are you serving him as well as you can in that role? Are you missing opportunities for personal spiritual growth? Are you missing opportunities for evangelizing others? You may have an opportunity for greater service to your faith by staying right where you are and simply becoming more faithful.

We are called to *be* the word of God in *all* we do. We can't just talk about it. We have to do it regardless of our current circumstance. A vivid example of this is conveyed in the experience of Cardinal François Xavier Van Thuân, who said this about his thirteen years of imprisonment during Vietnam's communist regime.

> After they arrested me in August 1975, two policemen took me by night from Saigon to Nha Trang, a 280-mile trip. So began my life as a prisoner, without timetables, without nights or days. [My] heart felt lacerated by the remoteness of my people. In the darkness of the night, in the midst of that ocean of anxiety, of nightmare, little by little I began to awaken: "I must face reality. I am in prison. Isn't this, perhaps, the best time to do something great? How many times in my life will I have such an opportunity again? The only sure thing in life is death. Therefore, *I must take advantage of the occasions that come my way each day to carry out ordinary actions in an extraordinary way.*"
>
> …During the long nights of pressure, *I convinced myself that to live the present moment is the simplest and surest way to reach sanctity.* This conviction inspired a prayer: "*Jesus, I will not wait,*

I want to live this present moment filling it with love." The straight line is made up of millions of little points joined to one another. My life is also made up of millions of seconds and minutes joined among themselves. If I live each second [deliberately], the line will be straight. *If I live each minute perfectly, life will be saintly.*[35]

If each of us strives for this level of sanctification, the results we will produce will be nothing short of magnificent. We start small, with one step, and then we string together days and weeks.

Setting our own lives on a path toward enlightenment begins with a commitment to fill each moment with the fullness of God's love and to take advantage of the occasions that come our way each day to carry out ordinary actions in an extraordinary way. St. Paul says: "Do all things without grumbling or questioning, that you may be blameless and innocent, children of God without blemish *in the midst of a crooked and perverse generation*—among whom you shine like lights in the world, holding fast the word of life" (Philippians 2:14, emphasis added).

St. Peter warns us: "Be sober, be watchful. Your adversary the devil prowls around like a roaring lion, seeking someone to devour. Resist him, firm in your faith, knowing that the same experience of suffering is required of your brotherhood throughout the world" (1 Peter 5:8–9).

Today we live in a post-Christian—even an *anti*-Christian—world. Not to understand this cripples us as individuals and weakens our Church community. Many around us feel a sense of uncertainty; they are disoriented and hopeless, and this even includes Christians.

We are all, at least partially, products of the time in which we live. The challenges of being Catholic today are different than the challenges Christians faced in ancient Rome, during the Dark Ages, or during World War II. The challenges of our times, therefore, make different demands on us than those that were placed on Catholics in previous eras. The demands faced by Catholics today were again outlined by Archbishop Chaput in his Philadelphia address. They include the following:

First, we must all be leaders in our faith. We must be leaders in our homes, in our parishes, our workplaces, and the broader communities in which we live. We need to lead first by example, as Jesus did. As St. Francis of Assisi is thought to have said, "Preach the gospel daily, but only use words if you must." As devoted Catholics we will be under the spotlight more than others. We must ensure that anytime the spotlight shines our way, it reflects a solid representation of Catholic teaching, both in our words *and* our deeds.

Second, we must understand the issues of the day in the context of Catholic teaching. According to Archbishop Chaput the central issue of modern American life is the temptation to *accommodate, compromise, get along, and fit in*—and then to feel good about it. We accept *tepidness* in the name of *pluralism*. We put *diversity of belief and behavior* above *truth*. We put the *individual* above the *common good*. We put *tolerance* above *love, justice, and real charity*. But none of this saves souls in the name of Jesus Christ. On the contrary, it provides people with alibis and leeches away their faith.

Third, we must understand and help others to understand what it means to be an authentic Catholic layperson in the twenty-first century. The lay vocation is not about being a lector, altar server, extraordinary minister of Holy Communion, ecclesial minister, or member of the parish council—although all these roles are important and should be honored and appreciated. The vocation of the Catholic laity—the Catholic Church at its best—is meant to penetrate all the various levels of society and convert the culture for Jesus Christ.

> We know we've been given the truth of the Gospel through no merit of our own. We need to proclaim it humbly and confidently even when other people object....

On the tenth anniversary of *Veritatis Splendor*, John Paul II
wrote, "Beyond all the cultural changes there are essential realities
that do not change; rather they find their ultimate foundation in
Christ, who is always the same, yesterday, today, and forever…
therefore, the fundamental reference of Christian morality is not
the culture of man, but the plan of God." [36]

Consider John 15:18–19: "If the world hates you, know that it has hated
me before it hated you. If you were of the world, the world would love
its own; but because you are not of the world, but I chose you out of the
world, therefore the world hates you."

And remember Archbishop Chaput's unflinching statement: "We
need to love the world, but we also need to shed any illusions about
the compatibility of the spirit of our age and the spirit of Jesus. *They are
enemies.*"

We know that the cross of Jesus will triumph, but what does that mean?
Pope Benedict XVI, when he was still Cardinal Joseph Ratzinger, tackled
the question of how Christians should understand the triumph of Christ's
cross by referring to Jesus's promise that the gates of hell will not prevail
against the Church. The pope said this promise should be considered in
the light of Christ's question: "When the Son of Man comes, will he find
faith on earth?" (Luke 18:8).

It's valuable to study the life of St. John the Baptist, whose unique
purpose in life was to clear a path for the Messiah. He belonged to a
Jewish sect that dedicated their lives to prepare the way for the coming of
the Savior, as did the Blessed Virgin Mary and her parents.

We don't know the mind of God, but we do know that the victory of
Christ began with his resurrection and ascension to God's right hand.
What are we doing—you and I—to make sure that Christ finds great
faith when he returns in glory? We are the clearers of God's path during
our time.

Recall the words of the Canticle of Zechariah:

> And you, child, will be called the prophet of the Most High;
> for you will go before the Lord to prepare his ways,
> to give knowledge of salvation to his people
> in the forgiveness of their sins,
> through the tender mercy of our God
> when the day shall dawn upon us from on high,
> to give light to those who sit in darkness and in the shadow of
> death,
> to guide our feet into the way of peace. (Luke 1:76–79)

It is because of our role as twenty-first–century leaders that we must accept *the fourth requirement: We must settle for nothing less than magnificence.* If we are here to serve God, then magnificence is the only acceptable standard. That, of course, is obvious and should be sufficient reason for us to follow the example of Cardinal Thuân, who challenged us to take advantage of the occasions that come our way each day to carry out ordinary actions in an extraordinary way. This is a means to achieve personal sanctity.

But we will all be more effective if we are magnificent. In talking about the New Evangelization, Bl. John Paul II said, "Do not be satisfied with mediocrity."[37] Why? At least in part because those we want to influence will be more open to God's word if they are confronted with magnificence rather than mediocrity.

When people look at us as individuals, they should see God at work in our lives. It's the only way we can be authentic apostles in the modern world.

What, then, is the secret of personal magnificence? It is integrating all three dimensions of the human trinity on the strongest possible foundation of faith by clearly defining your faith purpose.

Define Your Faith Purpose

In recalling the Church teaching that our basic purpose is "to know, to love, and to serve God in this life and to be happy with him forever in the next," we find that our faith purpose consists of two parts. The first part is directed inward and focuses on our personal spiritual formation. This is how we know and love God. The second component focuses outward on worldly impact (helping to evangelize or to assist others in their spiritual formation). If we know and love God through our own spiritual growth and serve him through our service to others in charity, the result will be eternal happiness.

The next step in defining your purpose is to write a personal faith purpose statement that will serve you and others when it is achieved.

Examples of faith purpose statements:

> "As an authentic Catholic in the twenty-first century, one of my primary purposes in life is to learn, live, and spread the teachings of Jesus Christ in everything I do."

> "As a Catholic wife, mother, and school teacher, my role is to serve as a magnificent example of Jesus's teachings in everything I do each day."

> "My purpose is to be such a vivid example of the gospel in everything I do that I will inspire others to likewise seek eternal happiness by following in Jesus's footsteps."

> "As husband and wife we aspire to model our lives after Joseph and Mary and, through our example, inspire others to do the same."

Note that in several of the above examples certain key elements are included by implication, even though they are not explicitly stated. For example, in saying "I want to be a vivid example of the gospel in everything I do," it is implied that I must continually learn and study the gospel to accomplish this, even though it is not stated. Likewise, a couple that actively emulates Mary and Joseph seeks out Scripture stories and Catholic literature on the Holy Family. They may tape a holy card near their bed to recall their model every morning. They try to provide themselves with as many guideposts as possible.

We encourage you to write several different faith purpose statements to begin with. Think about them for several days, editing and rewriting them as you reflect. Discuss them with your spiritual advisor and other trusted confidants. During this period of discernment, with input from others, gradually refine your thinking until you have created a single statement you can wholeheartedly embrace. Then write this final faith purpose statement on a three-by-five card. Eventually you'll also write family and work purpose statements on three-by-five cards as well. Once they are all compiled, you can then carry them with you so you can easily to refer to them during times of prayer and meditation. Spell out your goal as simply and precisely as possible, and then let your words center you.

A final point in summarizing the importance of defining your faith purpose and remembering the role of God's graces in your life is best stated in the words of St. John of the Cross:

> When God beholds the soul made attractive through grace, he is impelled to grant her more grace, for he dwells within her well pleased with her... Because this grace exalts, honors, and beautifies her in his sight, God loves her ineffably. If prior to her being in grace, he loved her only on account of himself, now that she is in grace he loves her not only on account of himself but also on account of herself. And thus enamored by means of the effects and works of grace, or without them, he ever continues to communicate more love and more graces. And as he continues

to honor and exalt her, he becomes continually more captivated by and enamored of her.[38]

Isn't that encouraging? Grace begets grace. Do whatever you can to put your soul in that state and reap boundless blessings.

> God manifests this in speaking to his friend Jacob through Isaiah: "Because you are precious in my eyes, / and honored, and I love you" (Isaiah 43:4). In other words, after God turned his eyes upon Jacob, thus giving him grace and making him glorious and worthy of honor and God's presence, Jacob merited the grace of more of God's favors.
>
> It is better to limp along the way than stride along off the way. For a man who limps along the way, even if he only makes slow progress, comes to the end of the way; but one who is off the way, the more quickly he runs, the further away he is from his goal. If you are looking for a goal, hold fast to Christ, because He Himself is the Truth, where we desire to be … hold fast to Christ if you wish to be safe. [39]
>
> —St. Thomas Aquinas

CHAPTER SIXTEEN

Discern Your Family Purpose

The headline hit us hard: a February 17, 2012, *New York Times* article titled "For Women Under 30, Most Births Occur Outside Marriage." For some time we had been sobered by the statistic that four in ten U.S. babies are born to unwed parents. Then came this news, a turning point of epic proportions: More than half of births to American women under thirty now occur outside marriage. "It used to be called illegitimacy," the article written by Jason DeParle and Sabrina Tavernise began. "Now it is the new normal." An accompanying photo showed Teresa Fragoso, a young woman with big brown eyes and a somber expression, who works at an Ohio bar, where she one day took her son when she could not find a sitter.

The research about what kind of future awaits these children is unequivocal. "According to the U.S. Center for Disease Control, 85% of all children exhibiting behavior disorders come from fatherless homes. Studies going back a quarter century show that 80% of rapists and 70% of juveniles in state-operated institutions are from fatherless homes."[40] Adolescents, particularly boys, in single-parent families are at higher risk of committing crimes. Moreover, students attending schools with a high proportion of single parents are also at risk. Youths are more at risk of first drug use without a highly involved father. Each unit increase in father involvement is associated with a 1 percent reduction in substance use. Living in an intact family decreases the risk of first substance abuse.[41]

According to Patrick Fagan, the William H.G. FitzGerald Fellow at the Heritage Foundation, "When you control for marriage, the crime rates between blacks and whites show no difference."[42] In other words, if you compare crime rates between black and white families with two married parents and black and white families without two married parents, the statistics don't vary across racial lines. It is the family relationship that makes the difference, not race. It is unfortunate that sociologists are just now beginning to examine the correlations between family, fatherhood, and the overall health and well-being of our society. On the other hand, we should appreciate that they are finally starting to explain what Catholics have always known: Healthy family environments with strong father role models lead to a healthy social environment.

Sociologist Bradford Wilcox, author of the book *Soft Patriarchs*, is one researcher able to explain why this is true. "Boys that grow up in fatherless homes engage in compensatory masculinity," he said. "They try to separate themselves from their mothers, yet prove their masculinity by being more aggressive, more violent and more sexually active. Without an appropriate model in the home, they do not learn the appropriate clues."[43]

"Wilcox added that the role of a father is indispensable. Nonresidential dads, such as an uncle or Big Brother, cannot easily fill in for a missing father.

" 'They tend to treat kids to a movie or a sporting event.' said Wilcox. 'That's not really what kids need from men. They need men who can challenge them, discipline them and show them how to handle stress.'"[44]

David Pence, a Catholic physician who also serves as editor of *City Fathers* magazine in Minneapolis, cites 1980 as the end of a thirty-year breakdown of civic order, not only in Minneapolis, but also in most of urban America. For example, in Minneapolis in 1950 there were 140,000 *more* people, 400 *fewer* rapes, 40 *fewer* murders, and 3,000 *fewer* burglaries than in 1980. Furthermore, the population was poorer and denser in 1950. This period was the de-Christianization of certain segments of society and there were 500 *fewer* police officers. What happened during desacralization of marriage? He goes on to say that "crime is the result of a lack of socialization of males"[45] *within the family* and among other social groups in society. He makes a strong case that one of the most important factors in eliminating crime is to restore both a solid religious framework and a respect for marriage and family.

But the problem is not merely a male problem. Girls raised in fatherless families can suffer consequences every bit as devastating. *Los Angeles Magazine* recently chronicled the story of an eighteen-year-old woman deeply embedded in the porn industry, sometimes being filmed in up to four pornographic films per week. Her father left home when she was under the age of ten. She started watching porn on the Internet at age eleven, became sexually active a short time later, and carried on a perverted relationship with an older man at age seventeen. As soon as she turned eighteen, she moved to Los Angeles and began making porn films that are especially degrading and demeaning.[46] One can't help but think that in having her fatherly role model replaced by the Internet, the outcome was predictable. Although not all women from broken homes end up on such a destructive path, many suffer lifelong negative consequences of low self-esteem and underachievement.

With all these negative consequences to individuals and to society at large, how then do we put the issue of today's family in perspective? We start with a message from Pope John Paul II.

> In a world that is becoming ever more secularized, the great task of the believing family is to become conscious of its own vocation and mission. In every circumstance, the starting point for this work is to safeguard and intensify *prayer, an unceasing prayer to*

the Lord to increase one's faith and make it more vigorous....

It is true that, when one goes through difficult times, the support of science can be of great help, but nothing can replace an ardent, personal, and confident faith that is open to the Lord, who said, "*Come to me, all you who labour and are heavy burdened and I will give you rest*" (Matthew 11:28).

The indispensable source of energy and renewal, when frailty and weakness increase, is the encounter with the living Christ, Lord of the Covenant. This is why you must develop an intense spiritual life and open your soul to the Word of life. In the depths of the heart the voice of God must be heard, even if at times it seems to be silent, in reality it resounds continually in the heart and accompanies us along the path that can have its burden of sorrow....

Special care must be shown to young spouses so that they do not surrender in the face of problems and conflicts. Prayer, frequent recourse to the sacrament of reconciliation, spiritual direction, must never be abandoned with the idea that one can replace them with other techniques of human and psychological support. We must never forget what is essential, namely, to live in the family under the tender and merciful gaze of God.

The richness of the sacramental life, in the life of the family that participates in the Eucharist every Sunday, is undoubtedly the best antidote for confronting and overcoming obstacles and tensions.

This is even more necessary when there abound lifestyles, fashion and cultures that bring into doubt the value of the marriage, even reaching the point of holding that it is impossible to realize the mutual gift of self in marriage until death in joyful fidelity. Human frailty grows if the divorce mentality dominates....

There is no difficult situation that cannot be adequately confronted when one cultivates a genuine atmosphere of Christian life. Love itself, wounded by sin, is still a redeemed love. It is clear that, if sacramental life is weak, the family yields more easily to snares because it is deprived of any defences.

How important it is to foster family support for couples, especially young couples, by families who are spiritually and morally solid. It is a fruitful and necessary apostolate at this time in history.[47]

The Extent of Our Family Responsibility

Each of us has a dual family responsibility. We have responsibilities to the family we were born into and to the family we create. To achieve this dimension of our calling, unless we are called to remain single as laypersons, we either marry another person for the purpose of procreation or we choose to marry the Church. Because this decision will have a profound impact on how a person carries out the faith and work dimensions of adulthood, it should be resolved first.

Marriage and Holy Orders are sacraments based on a permanent covenant with God. A person chooses one or the other as the result of a discerning process that frames that person's spousal calling for life. This decision informs each of us about who our spouse will be and how we will fulfill the spousal dimension of our family calling here on earth.

In addition to the spousal dimension of family, we also have a calling to serve both the families we were born into and the ones we create. Good sons and daughters respect and honor their parents through the holy witness of their life. Real brothers and sisters support their brothers and sisters. Genuine parents nurture their children and serve as valid role models in everything they do. We cannot expect to serve our Lord with a lack of fraternal charity or the absence of real, sacrificial love for our parents, our siblings, and our offspring. In fact, the *Catechism* says it is possible to achieve this service to family without marrying. Paragraph 2231 states: "Some forego marriage in order to care for their parents or brothers and sisters, to give themselves more completely to a profession, or to serve other honorable ends. They can contribute greatly to the good of the human family."

Only after we have framed our life through determination of our faith and family calling can we begin to discern our work purpose. Our work purpose comprises all the things we do, both paid and unpaid, that make the world a better place. In chapter seventeen we cover how to discern your work purpose.

But it is important to remember here that faith, family, and work are not mutually exclusive dimensions of our lives. One of the most common mistakes people make is to think that the time they spend on the job or going to work is time separate from family or faith. This causes them to become clock-watchers or time card punchers, counting the seconds until they complete the absolute minimum amount of time required for work so they can devote time to family or faith. They resent any overtime or extra effort required by their employer. In other words, they lose sight of the fact that the job provides economic well-being for the family and an opportunity to honor God through the development and effective use of their natural gifts. If you occasionally put in extra effort on the job that leads to recognition, advancement, and pay raises, aren't you also serving your family by providing greater benefits, rewards, and comfort? Of course you are.

Measure your commitment to both family and work not by time spent but by *impact*. Regularly ask: "What benefits am I bringing to my family through the work that I do?" "How does my work benefit from the family conditions we maintain?" "How does my faith affect both family and work?" The more you can get the concentric circles of faith, family, and work to overlap in your life, the more fulfilled you will become.

For now, though, let's focus on clarifying one's family purpose by asking: "What are the purposes of family?" Then you can better answer the question: "What should my family purpose be?"

Family Purpose in Perspective

The Church begins by teaching us that family members "are persons equal in dignity" and that "for the common good of its members and of society, the family necessarily has manifold responsibilities, rights, and duties."

The role of the family can be further understood through the *Catechism*:

> The Christian family constitutes a specific revelation and realization of ecclesial communion, and for this reason it can and should be called a domestic church. It is a community of faith, hope, and charity; it assumes singular importance in the Church, as is evident in the New Testament. (*CCC*, 2204)[48]

> The Christian family is a communion of persons, a sign and image of the communion of the Father and the Son in the Holy Spirit. In the procreation and education of children it reflects the Father's work of creation. It is called to partake of the prayer and sacrifice of Christ. Daily prayer and the reading of the Word of God strengthen it in charity. The Christian family has an evangelizing and missionary task. (*CCC*, 2205)

> The relationships within the family bring an affinity of feelings, affections and interests, arising above all from the members' respect for one another. The family is a privileged community

called to achieve "a sharing of thought and common deliberation by the spouses as well as their eager cooperation as parents in the children's upbringing." (*CCC*, 2206)[49]

The family is the original cell of social life. It is the natural society in which husband and wife are called to give themselves in love and in the gift of life. Authority, stability, and a life of relationships within the family constitute the foundations for freedom, security, and fraternity within society. The family is the community in which, from childhood, one can learn moral values, begin to honor God, and make good use of freedom. Family life is an initiation into life in society. (*CCC*, 2207)

Families have a purpose to serve their members, to evangelize and educate, and to serve society. History has validated time and time again the Catholic teaching that the family is the original cell of social life. The strength of a society rests on the strength of its families. What then, are the responsibilities of family members to ensure the family achieves its purpose? Let's examine our duties as children first.

Our Duties as Catholic Children

The Church teaches that whether children are minors or adults, they are required by God's commandment to respect their parents. This respect, called *filial piety*, evolves from the gratitude for the parents, who through the gifts of life, love, and work have brought the children into the world and enabled them to grow in stature, wisdom, and grace.

With all your heart honor your father, and do not forget the birth pangs of your mother. Remember that through your parents you were born; what can you give back to them that equals their gift to you? (*CCC*, 2215)[50]

The Church further teaches that filial respect should promote harmony in all of family life, which means it also concerns relationships between brothers and sisters (see *CCC*, 2219). As family members, each of us carries the responsibility to cultivate and maintain loving, harmonious relationships with our siblings. This can be more difficult as we grow up and grow apart, sometimes questioning each other's decisions, but keeping the peace is nonnegotiable, according to the Church.

Our Duties as Catholic Parents

The Church teaches that our roles as parents extend beyond the procreation of children to include the responsibilities of moral education and spiritual formation. "The role of parents in education is of such importance that it is almost impossible to provide an adequate substitute. The right and duty of parents to educate their children are primordial and inalienable" (*CCC*, 2221). [51]

Parental duties and responsibilities are among the most important of our obligations (see *CCC*, 2223; 2228). It is within the boundaries of these responsibilities that you can then define a more specific individual purpose for yourself.

Identifying Your Purpose in Regard to Family

Your family purpose statement will most likely have a double focus. It will address both the family you were born into and the family you have created or will create. You will also want it to take into account your various roles, (i.e., sibling, husband, wife, father, or mother). It might also take into account your stage of life. Your purpose (and especially the activities you carry out to fulfill your purpose) might be different in regard to your children when they are under the age of five than it is when they are mature adults.

Examples of family purpose statements:

"As the parents of Mary, John, and Elizabeth, our purpose is to provide for their spiritual, psychological, and intellectual growth as well as their physical well-being so that they may grow up with their souls in union with God and with the necessary foundation to respond to God's call for them in every possible way."

"As the mother of Susan, Katherine, Danny, Bob, Billy, and Jim, my purpose is to create a home environment that will allow them to become righteous and faith-filled adults, with confidence in their God-given gifts so they may serve God and humanity in a manner that is pleasing to God."

"As the son of Dorothy, my purpose is to love, respect, and care for her during her final years so she may pass from this world to the next in a peaceful manner with love in her heart and the confidence she will gain eternal happiness with God."

As you did in discerning your faith purpose, we encourage you to write several statements to begin with. Think about them for several days, editing and rewriting them as you reflect. Discuss them with your spouse and other trusted advisors. During this period of discernment, gradually refine your thinking until you have created a single statement you can wholeheartedly embrace. Write this final family purpose statement on a three-by-five card similar to the one on which you wrote your faith purpose. Eventually you'll also write a work purpose statement on a three-by-five card as well.

Philip Rivers, quarterback of the San Diego Chargers, is a devout Catholic who profoundly understands his purpose in life. He often talks about the three Fs that anchor him: Faith, Family, and Football. He is a wise, successful man whose concentric circles overlap considerably. Being a father to six children helps him put his NFL career in perspective, he said in an interview with the Couple to Couple League for its magazine, *Family Foundations*:

> When I come home I'm able to be a husband and a dad. It keeps you grounded, not so much constantly getting caught up in what's on Sports Center and what people are saying. For me, there's nothing better than coming home from a road game— win or lose, but losing, more than anything, it helps me get over a loss and move to the next game—and pulling in the driveway and there are bicycles and scooters and side-walk chalk scattered all over the driveway. I get to come home to this. They all think Dad's the best, and they don't know if I threw two interceptions or if we won and everybody loves me, but they do.[52]

CHAPTER SEVENTEEN

Discern Your Work Purpose

How is work defined? Consider this answer, given by Gregory F.A. Pierce in his book *Spirituality at Work*:[53]

> *The Oxford English Dictionary* gives the noun *work* thirty-four
> different meanings and the verb thirty-nine. Do we mean only
> paid employment? What about all the volunteer work people
> do for free? What if someone is involuntarily unemployed or
> retired? The economists often want to equate work with paid
> employment, but most people's experience is that much of their
> daily work is unpaid, unrecognized, and often performed far
> away from the "marketplace."

Popular culture presents work as, at best, a tedious distraction, and, at worst, a "rat race" which—in the words of comedian Lily Tomlin—"even if you win, you're still a rat." (If you don't agree, try thinking of ten movies or television shows that portray work in a positive way—then eliminate those that are about teachers, medical personnel, parents, or a very few other service jobs.)

The prevailing view is that some work may be meaningful and fulfilling but most is not. While it is acknowledged that some people may love their work and feel they are helping others, it is thought that these people are few and far between and that most of them are either highly paid white-collar workers or in the helping professions. The perception is that for most people work is alienating, oppressive, exhausting—anything but spiritual.

But I think it is precisely because the workplace is often not spiritual by nature that what work needs more than anything else is an authentic spirituality. So let's try this definition of work:

> Work is all the effort (paid or unpaid) we exert to make the world a better place, a little closer to the way God would have things.

Under this definition all work—our jobs; fixing and cleaning up our homes; our church and community involvement; caring for parents, children, relatives, friends, and strangers; even some of our hobbies—can be seen in a spiritual light. Likewise, the toll collector on the expressway or the sanitation worker picking up the garbage has as much opportunity to discover the presence of God in the workplace as the lawyer or the nurse or the businessperson.

This definition—"work is all the effort (paid or unpaid) we exert to make the world a better place, a little closer to the way God would have things"—might cause you to change the way you think about your work. If you're one who has previously held negative attitudes about work, we hope it will change your attitude to one that is more positive.

Notice the all-inclusive nature of this definition. It also honors the work of being a parent, relative, or friend—helping a neighbor clean a gutter or sending a handwritten thank-you note to a godparent.

Catholics and Work

Catholic teachings place great value on both work and workers. The *Catechism* says the following about work:

The development of social activity and growth in production are meant to provide for the needs of human beings. Economic life is not meant solely to multiply goods produced and increase profit or power; it is ordered first of all to the service of persons, of the whole of man, and of the entire human community. Economic activity, conducted according to its own proper methods, is to be exercised within the limits of the moral order, in keeping with social justice so as to correspond to God's plan for man (*CCC*, 2426).[54]

Human work proceeds directly from persons created in the image of God and called to prolong the work of creation by subduing the earth, both with and for one another. Hence work is a duty: "If any one will not work, let him not eat." **Work honors the Creator's gifts and the talents received from him.** It can also be redemptive. By enduring the hardship of work in union with Jesus, the carpenter of Nazareth and the one crucified on Calvary, man collaborates in a certain fashion with the Son of God in his redemptive work. He shows himself to be a disciple of Christ by carrying the cross, daily, in the work he is called to accomplish. **Work can be a means of sanctification and a way of animating earthly realities with the spirit of Christ** (*CCC*, 2427). [55]

In work, the person exercises and fulfills in part the potential inscribed in his nature. The primordial value of labor stems from man himself, its author and its beneficiary. Work is for man, not man for work.

Everyone should be able to draw from work the means of providing for his life and that of his family, and of serving the human community (*CCC*, 2428, emphasis added).

One of the most important concepts regarding Catholic theology and work is that no matter how much our work focuses on exterior activity, authentic Catholics never allow this activity to separate us from intimate union with God. Rather, our union with God is meant to blossom from all our activities, including our work. Authentic Catholics don't limit their union with God to their hours of prayer. Instead, they strive to create a permanent and indissoluble union that embraces every moment of their lives, including their work lives.

Our work should be a prayer—an offering. But it can only be so if the work stems from one who is intimately tied to God while performing its activities. Jesus said, "As the branch cannot bear fruit by itself, unless it abides in the vine, neither can you, unless you abide in me" (John 15:4).

Union with God is the indispensable requirement for the efficacy of anyone's work. This union is accomplished by means of sanctifying grace, grows through receiving the sacraments and by practicing the virtues, and is strengthened through prayer. The more one's union with God increases while working, the more the actions that flow from it will bear fruit for souls. Work activity that is purely external—especially activity conducted under the pretext of having important duties while neglecting the importance for prayer and the quest for union with God's graces—condemns itself to sterility.

Meaningful work demands sacrifice—sometimes because of the fatiguing effort it imposes, sometimes because of its continual contact with people of different tastes, mentalities, or habits, and sometimes because it can expose us to the possibility of failure. Authentic Catholics accept all these challenges with a generous heart, convinced that from them will come the fruit of God's works. To be an authentic Catholic means that all works, and the way we carry them out, must be undertaken solely in service to God and in a manner that conforms to his will.

We yearn to live integrated lives, and this is how we do so: Sunday mornings that somehow inform Monday mornings, prayer that carries over from the liturgy to the workweek. What is the value of committing oneself to God during Mass or evening prayer if, when doing our work, we commit ourselves to purely human activity that could be done by any professional or working person? Even nonbelievers devote themselves to social work: They open schools and hospitals, they print books and newspapers, and they spread propaganda. As authentic Catholics, we should distinguish ourselves by the interior spirit that animates our passion: the spirit created by fully internalizing God's grace. Only this spirit has the power to transform human activity into supernatural action worthy of God's call for each of us.

Define Your Work Purpose

Keeping in mind that your work purpose will guide you along with your faith and family purposes, write a personal work purpose that will serve to move you in the direction of God's call for you when it is fulfilled. Remember that it should take into account your gifts and what you have learned from personal experience thus far in your life.

Another thought to keep in mind in regard to work purpose comes from Andreas Widmer, former Swiss Guard member and global entrepreneur who wrote *The Pope and the CEO: John Paul II's Leadership Lessons to a Young Swiss Guard*. In an interview on *The Catholic Business Hour,* he said, "Our overarching goal at work shouldn't be to *make* more. It should be to *become* more."[56]

Examples of work purpose statements:

"As a letter carrier, my primary work purpose is to serve humankind by delivering important information and goods to people in such a manner that they are inspired by my example to pursue paths of true love and charity in their own hearts."

"As an engineer, my primary work purpose is to use my God-given gifts of creativity and problem solving to derive solutions to complex problems encountered in my industry in a way that encourages respect among others for all people."

"As a businessman, my purpose is to serve people through the sale of furniture and other home goods in a manner that pleases both my customers and God."

"As a doctor, my purpose is to heal and provide physical, psychological, and spiritual guidance and comfort to my patients so they may achieve optimal health in the eyes of God."

Follow the same process you used in writing your faith and family purpose statements. Write several different versions to begin with. Think about them for several days, editing and rewriting them as you reflect. Discuss them with other businesspeople and colleagues (including your spouse, if you are married) and gradually refine your thinking until you have created a single statement you can wholeheartedly embrace. Then write this final work purpose on its own three-by-five card. When completed, you will now have three such cards to carry with you to refer to while praying or meditating. These will help you to keep your focus, reminding you of your life's priorities and where to place your life's energy.

Review the cards at least once a year. Ask yourself if you have spent your time and energy on the right activities. Are you accomplishing your purpose? Or are you wasting time and energy on meaningless activities?

A key to making the most productive use of the time you have been given to live your life is to specifically assess whether or not you are spending it on meaningful activities. The way to know whether or not activities are meaningful is to ask whether or not they contribute to the fulfillment of your purpose.

For we are God's fellow workers…

—1 Corinthians 3:9

CHAPTER EIGHTEEN

Plan to Answer Your Call

Now that you have identified your call and your unique gifts, it's time to determine how you will answer the call they point to.

Even though the following planning process separates your call into three separate components—faith, family, and work—the overarching goal here is to integrate them all into one.

Plan for Fulfilling Your Faith Purpose

Some people balk when we talk to them about planning their faith life. They think it sounds too formal or businesslike. "Faith is something you either have or you don't," they say. "Planning for it seems kind of silly, or at the least out of place." We disagree and here's why.

We've seen too many people who, by not planning (and thereby not prioritizing) their life's activities, let their commitment to their faith slip. By not committing to participate in faith-related activities, they allow other activities to take their place. For example, consider Sunday Mass attendance. Attendance shouldn't be seen as a choice, but as a given. Failure to attend constitutes a mortal separation from God. However, if I plan on going to church this weekend, I'll probably go. I certainly have a greater likelihood than if I don't plan on it and leave it to chance. If I plan to attend a specific Mass at a specific church, then I have an even higher likelihood that I'll attend.

If I plan my day so that I set aside certain times of the day for prayer, I have a much higher likelihood of praying that day than if I simply say that I'll pray "when I get a chance." I give myself a leg up by building it into my day or weaving it into a morning or evening ritual; it might be as simple as a Hail Mary while brushing my teeth.

Even though participation in the Eucharist and regular prayer are top priorities, there are other faithful activities that are more likely to happen if you plan for them to happen and less likely to happen if you don't. Therefore, you should plan.

Some of the things you should plan for include: weekly and daily Mass attendance, time for prayer and meditation, time to read and learn more about the faith, time devoted to the other sacraments (especially reconciliation), time for evangelization, and time for helping others learn and grow in faith. In fact, one way to set goals and plan in this department of your life is to conduct a simple audit of how you have been spending your time in these types of activities. A short form for conducting such an audit is presented in figure 18.1.

Figure 18.1. Faith Activity Self-Audit

The purpose of this self audit is to help you gain insight about how much of your time is devoted to fulfilling your faith purpose. Put an X on the line that best describes your participation in the list of faith-based activities.

	Excellent	Could Improve
Attend Mass every Sunday?	_____	_____
Attend daily Mass?	_____	_____
Participate in reconciliation frequently?	_____	_____
Pray the rosary often?	_____	_____
Pray novenas for special intentions?	_____	_____
Set aside time for morning prayer?	_____	_____

Say grace before every meal?	_____	_____
Pray before commencing work?	_____	_____
Pray before starting special projects?	_____	_____
Dedicate time to learning more about your faith?	_____	_____
Dedicate time to helping others grow their faith?	_____	_____
Dedicate time to evangelize?	_____	_____
Make your work a prayer?	_____	_____
Make your daily activities a prayer?	_____	_____

Take a few minutes to complete the audit for yourself. You may react the way others have by saying, "Wait a minute. There are only two responses—'Excellent' and 'Could Improve.'" Remember the words of John Paul II: "Mediocrity is not an option." When it comes to your faith, your practices either meet a standard of excellence or they could stand improvement. Jesus also strongly rejected mediocrity. "Because you are lukewarm, and neither cold nor hot," Revelation 3:16 tells us, "I will spew you out of my mouth."

Once you've completed the audit, then set goals to make changes in your life that will improve your practices over time. You don't have to change every thing at once. For example, if you have only four Xs in the "Excellent" column and twelve in the "Could Improve" column, don't feel as though you must immediately change all twelve of those answers. Pick the top one or two and set a goal to work on those during the next month. Then pick two more, and so on, until you score reasonably well. Or pick three or four to work on during the next three months, and then reassess. The most important thing is that you are honest with yourself and that you use the audit as a planning tool to improve your faithfulness over time.

After completing the audit, review your faith purpose statement and set two or three goals. Determine the time frame during which you want to achieve those goals. Write them in the following format:

To *(followed by an action or accomplishment verb)*
(state a single key result)
by *date*
at *cost*

Following this format, a clear definition of a goal a person might set in response to a concern uncovered by the audit might be:

To *attend Mass every Sunday and at least three times during the week*
at *a cost of six hours of my time per week*

Another example might be:

To *teach religious education classes one evening per week during the school year*
at *a cost of four hours per week of my time*

The reason we include statements of cost in our goals is so that we are clear with ourselves from the beginning what level of commitment we must make in order to satisfy our intentions. Many people mistakenly set a goal without thinking through the investment. Then later on when they fall short of achieving the goal, they say, "I didn't realize it would take that much time (or money or effort)."

Examples of statements that would not be good goals might be:

"To be a better Catholic"

"To be more faithful"

While these are noble intentions, they are not valid goals because they are too ambiguous. They are not specific enough. What do they mean? How can you measure them? How do you know if you've accomplished them?

Once you've determined your faith goals, write them on a three-by-five card so you can carry them with you and review them regularly during times of meditation and prayer.

Plan for Fulfilling Your Family Purpose

You might think it sounds too businesslike or formal to plan family matters, feeling those should be more spontaneous. Like matters of faith, however, if you allow matters of family to "just happen," or to evolve spontaneously, they won't be nearly as fulfilling, nor will they likely be as special. Don't rely on spontaneity alone to provide the richness and full potential of your family. For example, let's say you're on a family road trip in California and you drive by one of the California missions founded by Junipero Serra back in the late 1700s. This would be a great opportunity to hop out of the car and visit the mission as a family. You'd learn about the California missions, see interesting artifacts, and gain an appreciation for California's earliest European settlers. But it's probably not wise to leave your entire road trip to chance discoveries. You'd probably want to plan in advance a trip to Disneyland, a visit to the beach, and maybe a stop at the world-famous San Diego Zoo.

Another way to think about this is that planning can help make family events more special. When you are scheduling a birthday party, for instance, ask, "How can we plan this party to make it extra special?" When our son, Chip, was four, he was enamored of fire trucks and firefighters. When we began planning his fifth birthday party, we contacted the nearest fire station and asked the fire chief if we could do something at the fire station for Chip's birthday party. He was more than happy to accommodate us, so we took fifteen five-year-olds to the fire station for a tour and an opportunity to climb in and out of the trucks, see them squirt their hoses, and learn how the sirens worked. The firefighters all enjoyed some birthday cake, and the kids had a blast, creating the memory of a lifetime. Because we planned it, we were able to make the event very special without added cost or effort. It's a party Chip still remembers to this day. Of course, the pictures of a bunch of five-year-olds wearing adult fire boots and trying to get into firefighter gear helped seal the memory forever.

Each year we set our goals for the following year during the week between Christmas and New Year's Day. We set goals for the family as a unit as well as for each member. We include recreational goals, such as vacations and birthday parties, developmental goals in areas such as education or personal skill development, health goals so we can stay healthy and vibrant, and spiritual goals so we can individually and collectively grow in our faith.

Setting these goals allows us to make better use of our time when it comes to family. For example, during the evening when we have free time to spend—periods that we call "gifts of time" to spend how we want—if we have goals we will almost always tend to choose to spend our time doing something that contributes to those goals. Rather than plop down on the couch and watch some mindless TV program, we'll engage in activities that are much more meaningful and productive.

Then, at the end of the week, when we look back and ask the question, "How well did we use the time that was available to us?" the answer is usually positive. We spent the discretionary time we had available doing the things that were most important to us. We didn't waste a lot of time pursuing meaningless activities. If we didn't have plans and goals, there is no way we could have spent our time productively, because we would have no criteria against which to evaluate our decisions.

You can conduct an audit with family-related pursuits the same way you did for faith-related pursuits. Again, use the following scorecard.

Figure 18.2. Family Activity Self-Audit

The purpose of this self audit is to help you gain insight about how much of your time is devoted to fulfilling your family purpose. Put an X on the line that best describes your participation in the list of family activities.

	Excellent	Could Improve
Spend quality time with family every day?	_____	_____
Make family activities extra special?	_____	_____
Help other family members grow their faith?	_____	_____
Pray the rosary as a family?	_____	_____
Have at least one family meal together daily?	_____	_____
Have family talks about faith?	_____	_____
Spend time nurturing each other's natural gifts?	_____	_____
Talk about each family member's goals?	_____	_____
Encourage each other in their endeavors?	_____	_____
Celebrate family members' successes?	_____	_____
Reinforce each other's uniqueness?	_____	_____
Attend Mass together?	_____	_____
Talk about the readings from Mass together?	_____	_____
Have family service projects?	_____	_____
Make family activities a prayer?	_____	_____
Pray for each other?	_____	_____

After completing the audit, review your family purpose statement and set two or three goals. As before, determine the time frame during which you want to achieve those goals. Also as before, write them in the following format:

To   *(followed by an action or accomplishment verb)*
      (state a single key result)

by   *date*

at   *cost*

Following this format, a clear definition of a goal a person might set in response to a concern they had regarding the family audit might be:

To *volunteer to be the scorekeeper for our son's Little League team this spring*

at *a cost of five hours of my time per week*

Another example might be:

To *take the family on an educational, one-week vacation this summer*

at *a cost of two weeks of my time (including planning and preparations) and $6,000*

Sometimes our statements of cost will include actual dollar amounts. Again this makes it clear from the beginning what level of commitment we must make in order to satisfy our intentions. It also causes us to determine where the money will come from. Will I set it aside, take it from savings, or borrow it? Again, thinking through the cost issues in advance will not only prevent frustration and irritation later on, but will also increase the likelihood that the goals will be achieved in the specified time frame. It helps you make a total, clear-eyed commitment.

Examples of statements that would not be good family goals might be:

"To be a better husband"

"To be a better mother"

Again, these statements might represent noble intentions, but they are not valid goals because they are too ambiguous. I can be a better husband simply by being grumpy one less time next week. Is that what you want? Be sure your goals point toward specific, identifiable accomplishments. Set yourself up for success!

As you did with your faith goals, once you've determined your family goals, write them on a three-by-five card so you can carry them with you and review them regularly during the day, and especially during times of meditation and prayer.

Plan for Fulfilling Your Work Promise

Once again, we'll encourage you to be proactive rather than reactive in how your approach your life's work. Don't be one of those people who start their career by getting a job and then allow the circumstances of that job to dictate their future opportunities and choices. We've found that the people who always scan the environment, reassess their own competencies and ambitions, and look ahead for new opportunities are always more successful and more fulfilled in the work arena than those who wait for opportunity to find them. This is true whether the work you do in your life is paid or unpaid.

In this day and age, it's wise for you to have a "Plan B." This is a backup plan or safety net you can turn to if something out of your control happens to your current job or career path.

It used to be that, for income–related work, people would find a job and stay with that company or organization until retirement. Those kinds of career paths are becoming increasingly less common. People are now changing jobs or careers several times during their careers. Quite often these changes are forced upon them by events such as corporate takeovers, bankruptcies, economic conditions requiring severe cost-cutting, or changes in market conditions. If events like this disrupt your work life (some would say *when* events like this disrupt your work life), you should have a plan to fall back on so you won't be left out in the cold.

If you are torn between two possible career path choices, consider developing them both and having one be your "A" plan and one your "B" plan. In today's world, you might pursue your "B" option sooner rather than later. Once again, take a hard look at your work-related tasks to determine if they are as prayerful and effective as they could be. Here's an audit to get you started:

Figure 18.3. Work Activity Self-Audit

The purpose of this self audit is to help you gain insight about how much of your time is devoted to fulfilling your work purpose. Put an X on the line that best describes your participation in the list of work activities.

	Excellent	Could Improve
Set goals for your career?	_____	_____
Regularly seek to better yourself?	_____	_____
Treat coworkers with dignity and respect?	_____	_____
Maintain the highest standards of integrity?	_____	_____
Maintain the highest standards of quality?	_____	_____
Help coworkers to do well?	_____	_____
Take good care of company property?	_____	_____
Set aside time for prayer during work?	_____	_____
Take good care of customers?	_____	_____
Pray before commencing work?	_____	_____
Pray before starting special projects?	_____	_____
Set a Christlike example for coworkers?	_____	_____
Practice the principles of servant leadership?	_____	_____
Avoid gossip about coworkers?	_____	_____
Make your work a prayer?	_____	_____
Make your daily activities on the job a prayer?	_____	_____

After completing the audit, review your work purpose statement and set two or three goals. As you did for faith and family, determine the time frame during which you want to achieve these goals. Once again, write your goals in the following format:

To *(followed by an action or accomplishment verb)*
    (state a single key result)
by *date*
at *cost*

Following this format, a clear definition of a goal a person might set in response to a concern uncovered in the audit might be:

To *identify a specific achievement I can accomplish during the next six months that will either solve a problem in my company or result in making the company better in some specific and tangible way, and then set a goal to accomplish it*
by *two weeks from today*
at *a cost of two hours of my time*

Another example might be:

To *review my resume with two other people to determine one or two things I can do next year to increase my value/worth to current or potential future employers, and then set a goal to do these things*
by *the first of the month*
at *a cost of three hours of my time*

The examples we used here are "enabling" goals as opposed to "end-result" goals. In essence, we've set a goal to set more goals. Some people might call these mere activities that lead to end-result goals. Either way, it is important that you focus your attention on setting end-result goals that are meaningful. Examples of end-result goals that might come from the two examples above include the following:

To *develop a simplified system for handling customer complaints that results in all complaints being resolved within forty-eight hours*
by *three months from today*
at *twelve hours of my time*

Another example might be:

To *complete a three-day workshop in customer service*

by *the end of September*

at *a cost of three days of my time, plus tuition and travel expenses (paid by company)*

After reading the first goal you might ask, "Where will the twelve hours come from?" This is a great question. You might go to your boss, explain you want to solve this problem, and ask for a few hours here and there to do it. But that might not be feasible, given workload or the requirements of your current position. So then what do you do? You bootleg the time, meaning you steal a few minutes here and there until the goal is accomplished. Maybe you work on it during a few lunch breaks, or come in early or stay late for a few days. Don't look at this as doing something for nothing. Rather, look at it as a short-term investment of your time and energy that will provide a long-term payoff. Pride yourself in pursuing this little secret, knowing it how rewarding it will be to complete. Once this achievement goes on your resume, no one can ever take it away.

Examples of statements that would not be good goals might be:

"To be a better employee"

"To work harder"

Once again, these are great intentions but lousy goals because they are too vague.

As you did for faith and family goals, when you've finished identifying and stating your work goals, write them on a three-by-five card so you can carry them with you and review them regularly throughout the day.

> The Lord answered me and said: "Write down the vision clearly upon the tablets, so that one can read it readily. For the vision still has its time, presses on to fulfillment, and will not disappoint. If it delays, wait for it, it will surely come, and not be late."
>
> —Habakkuk 2:2–3

CHAPTER NINETEEN

Use the Seven Virtues to Integrate God's Grace

The past few chapters have for the most part focused on "what." We've talked about what your skills and competencies are, and we've talked about what you should do with them in terms of God's call for you. Again, this is a "what" issue: What should I do with my life? This chapter addresses the issue of "how." *How* you do what you do is every bit as important as *what* you do.

It is easy to find examples of people who thought the ends justified the means. They created pure havoc, oftentimes along with misery and heartache, because they thought their end goal was so noble that anything they did in order to accomplish the goal was justified. For example, the Church's teaching on abortion is crystal clear and has been since the earliest writings of the apostles. We all share a key responsibility to fight for the rights of the unborn and protect life from the cradle to the grave. But *how* we fight for it makes a difference. It would be wrong to bomb abortion clinics and kill abortionists in pursuit of our goal.

There are right ways and wrong ways to go about everything—especially about how to pursue God's call for each of us. The seven virtues provide the most practical framework from which to look at *how* we should pursue our call. The *Catechism of the Catholic Church* specifies four human virtues (prudence, justice, fortitude, and temperance) and three theological virtues (faith, hope, and charity) that define how we should live our lives.[57] In medieval times the idea was that any person, whether Christian or not, might possess the four human virtues. But only a Christian would possess faith in God, hope for an afterlife, and the kind of charity in which one does good deeds out of love for God alone (*caritas*).

The *Catechism* introduces the four human virtues by saying, "Human virtues are firm attitudes, stable dispositions, habitual perfections of intellect that will govern our actions, order our passions, and guide our conduct according to reason and faith" (*CCC*, 1804). The phrases "govern our actions," "order our passions," and "guide our conduct" focus on the way we do things. They are more about how we go about using our unique gift mix to achieve our God-given mission in life than they are about what our mission should be.

The *Catechism* introduces the three theological virtues by saying, "The theological virtues are the foundation of Christian moral activity; they animate it and give it its special character. They inform and give life to all the moral virtues. They are infused by God into the soul of the faithful to make them capable of acting as his children and of meriting eternal life" (*CCC*, 1813). Again, please note the emphasis, with words such as activity, animate, and acting. These talk about the way we behave, which in turn focuses on how we do what we do as much as what it is we do.

Both how and what are important. But many writers who focus on helping people figure out their personal life's purpose spend most of their time focusing on determining the what and don't say much about the how. A very important aspect of integrating one's gifts effectively with one's purpose is to surround oneself with God's abundant grace. A practical and meaningful way to integrate God's grace in your life while answering God's call for you is to consistently make every effort possible to infuse the seven virtues in everything you do. It's at once a comprehensive and practical way to monitor your own behavior in order to ensure that you are seeking to do God's will by discerning the right purpose for your life *and* that you are also living in a manner that conforms to God's will in every action you take.

Use the Seven Virtues to Integrate God's Grace with Your Actions

Paragraph 1833 of the *Catechism of the Catholic Church* reiterates, "The human virtues are stable dispositions of the intellect and the will that govern our acts, order our passions, and guide our conduct in accordance with reason and faith." Let's examine each of the seven virtues in the specific context of answering God's call for us while exploring ways to use them to bring God's grace into our individual journeys.

Prudence

"Prudence disposes the practical reason to discern, in every circumstance our true good and to choose the right means for achieving it" (*CCC,* 1835). Prudence is the virtue that guides the other virtues by setting standards and boundaries. It directly brings our consciences to bear on judgments we make about different situations. It directs our conduct and applies moral judgments in different situations while in the process overcoming doubts about what good should be achieved and what evils should be avoided (see *CCC,* 1806). Let's examine several examples of the kind of circumstances where prudence might come into play while attempting to answer God's call.

Not long ago a caller phoned in to Dick's radio program.[58] The caller identified herself as a thirty-five-year-old woman who had discerned that she was being called to serve God more directly by entering a convent and becoming a nun. The only problem, she explained, was that she had accrued a fair amount of credit card debt, and the religious order wouldn't accept her until the debt was retired. The question she asked Dick was, "Is it a sin to get rid of my debt by declaring bankruptcy so I can enter the convent?"

How would you have answered this question? We've asked numerous people, and the variety of answers is interesting. Some take the position that the bankruptcy laws were established to help people out of a financial bind. They go on to say that businesses include these losses in their forecasts and profit estimates, so you're really not doing them any harm. Based on these premises, they would advise her to go ahead and declare bankruptcy.

Others suggested that she contact one of the companies that help people get out of debt by negotiating their debt with the creditors. One person even suggested simply walking away from it, leaving no forwarding address and changing her name when she entered the convent!

Dick's on the air answer was very different from those suggestions. He said that she had a moral obligation to repay the debt, because she had incurred it. She had given her word when she signed the credit card agreements. He suggested that she approach her pastor and the local chapter of Knights of Columbus at her parish and ask if they could help her with her debt so she could answer her call.

A young woman from our parish found herself in a similar situation a couple of years ago. The Knights stepped in, held a fundraiser, and raised enough money from everyone in the parish for her to be able to enter the convent. A year later, she returned to visit and spoke at every Mass, thanking the parishioners for their support and telling us about her first year in the convent. She talked about how rewarding it was and how she was more committed than ever to the call she had discerned. Her visit and her story lifted all of our hearts and helped us feel as though we had been able to exercise another virtue—charity—in a meaningful way that elevated us all.

Prudence often ensures that we don't take the easy but wrong path at the expense of a more difficult path that is aligned with God's grace. In the case of the aspiring nun, it would have been easy for her and everyone else to surmise that her goal was so noble that it justified almost any path to get there. That is never the case, however.

Justice

Again we turn to the *Catechism* for a definition. Paragraph 1836 states: "Justice consists in the firm and constant will to give God and their neighbor their due." Justice toward God is called the virtue of religion. The concept of justice toward others says that we should respect the rights of each person while seeking harmony and promoting equity with regard to people and the common good. Just people differentiate themselves by habitual right thinking and upright conduct toward their neighbors (see *CCC*, 1807).

Notice the use of the words *harmony* and *equity* as opposed to *equally* or *the same*. Not everyone is the same; therefore, it is hard to treat everyone equally. For example, if you were a shop supervisor, would you treat a forty-year-old, experienced worker with a track record of performing at the highest possible level of ability the same as an eighteen-year-old whose first day on the job was yesterday? If you did, you'd be a pretty lousy shop supervisor. However, would you treat the two equitably? The answer is a resounding yes. What exactly does this mean?

If the older, more experienced worker produces at high levels with minimal supervision, it makes sense to pay that person more based on productivity. But now let's assume it's time to determine bonuses. Let's further assume that both have demonstrated equal levels of effort, both have increased their knowledge and skill level, and both have comparable attendance, positive work relationships with others, and all the other factors that go into describing employees with good work habits. Let's say you determine that both should receive a 3 percent bonus for their efforts. Is this just? Remember that because their base pay is different, this means the older employee will actually receive more dollars than the younger one. Is this just? We believe it is, because you've applied the same percentage points to each. This makes it equitable, although not equal.

Almost everything in life is like this, if you think about it. Determining what is fair and what is not is always a challenge. This is one reason why prudence is usually listed as the first virtue. We must be prudent in order to be just.

Fortitude

Paragraph 1837 of the *Catechism* says "fortitude ensures firmness in difficulties and constancy in the pursuit of the good." In another section fortitude is described as helping to strengthen our resolve in resisting temptation and overcoming obstacles in our moral lives. It also allows us to overcome fear, including fear of death, and to face trials and persecutions, even to the extent of renouncing one's life for a just cause (see *CCC*, 1808).

Most of us won't be put in a situation where our lives are on the line in the defense of a just cause. But there are many circumstances where our careers or our jobs or what people perceive to be our reputations may be on the line. When we are on our chosen paths to answer God's call, our chosen calling should provide a tangible framework for making decisions about the different circumstances we encounter. Service to God and humankind should be at the top of our decision-making priorities. Consider the following example.

One morning when Dick was a young naval officer onboard a ship steaming in the South China Sea, he was slated to relieve the officer of the deck at 3:45 A.M. (The officer of the deck reports directly to the captain for the proper operation of the ship and is responsible for the overall operation and navigation of the ship). Upon arriving on the bridge early to prepare to take over, Dick realized that the ship had changed course two hours earlier to steam away from a sinking Taiwanese merchant ship from which they had received an SOS. This meant that Dick's ship was steaming in violation of Navy regulations, international law, and the international rules of the road, even though the captain had ordered the course change.

Dick was the most junior officer among all those qualified to be officers of the deck. The officer he was relieving was the most senior. He and the captain held Dick's future in their hands in a very competitive career environment. Should Dick go ahead and relieve the watch as they expected, or should he take the morally correct stand and refuse to relieve the watch, thereby confronting and alienating them both? What would you have done?

Dick refused to relieve the watch until the captain came to the bridge, had everything explained to him, and then gave Dick a direct order to relieve the watch. Needless to say, both the captain and the more senior watch officer were angry that Dick had taken the stand he did. Later on, the ship was ordered to render aid to the sinking ship, but it arrived too late. The ship had already gone down and twenty-five people died. One survivor was rescued. Dick had put his career on the line by standing up for what was morally right. Most of his peers chided him in private for taking a stand that in the end didn't save many lives and probably torpedoed his career.

As it turned out, however, the story came out, and Dick was the first in his class from the Naval Academy to be promoted to the rank of lieutenant (O3). He was promoted thirteen months ahead of his class and a month ahead of the class before him. Of course, that's not the real reward. The real reward is that Dick showed fortitude in serving the common good in spite of expected persecution and harassment.

Temperance

The Church teaches us that this is the virtue that "moderates the attraction of the pleasures of the senses and provides balance in the use of created goods" (*CCC*, 1838). Temperance ensures the will's mastery over instincts and keeps our desires within the limits of what is honorable (see *CCC*, 1809). Let's look at an example of how this might come into play when someone is answering their call.

A friend of ours, a very successful businesswoman, recently started a nonprofit organization to help fight the problem of human trafficking. Her vision was particularly vital because although she wanted to address the problem by getting laws changed in various countries to make it more difficult for traffickers, she also wanted her organization to focus specifically on rescuing and finding homes for victims of the sex trade under the age of sixteen. These homes would focus on safety and on training the young victims for various vocations so they could avoid getting trapped again into the lifestyle from which they had just been rescued.

Her problem was intemperance. She provided the initial funds for the project from her own savings and combined it with donations from a few friends. Because she was used to working in somewhat elegant surroundings, she decided to "set things up right" so her organization would look different from all the other nonprofits and "present an appearance" that conveyed success, confidence, and a businesslike approach, while making her feel good about her lavish surroundings. She spent a lot of money on extravagant office furnishings, paintings, brochures, stationery, business cards, and the like.

She also made one other mistake. She was used to traveling first class, and she continued to do so. When she dined on the road, she ate at high-priced, upscale restaurants, spending the organization's money on expensive meals for herself, rather than on furthering the organization's mission. Her attitude was, "I'm giving a lot to this cause. At my age, the least they do is let me travel the way I'm used to." You can imagine the reaction of potential donors. They all felt that if a nonprofit was spending money so extravagantly, it either didn't need donations, or it was simply not providing proper stewardship for the funds it had already received.

After a couple of years, the woman was forced to close the doors due to lack of funds. It is a shame she wasn't successful, because her call was extraordinarily noble. She failed because she lacked temperance in how she went about achieving her call. Remember, what you decide to do in answering God's call for you is important, but equally important to your success is how you decide to do it. If you don't surround yourself with virtue in everything you do, you are destined to fail.

It is also worth noting that, in this particular case, even though this woman's intentions were noble, her actions probably didn't bring her closer to eternal salvation—our ultimate goal—because in the end her impact on the common good was next to nothing. There's a bit of truth to that saying we've all heard hundreds of times before, "The road to hell is paved with good intentions." Lack of temperance is often the cause of many good intentions never being realized.

Faith

Faith means that "we believe in God and believe all that he has revealed to us and that Holy Church proposes for our belief" (*CCC*, 1842). It is through faith that people truly commit themselves to God. Faithful people always seek to know and to do God's will (see *CCC*, 1814).

A key element of the virtue of faith is that it involves *always* seeking to know and to do God's will. The operative word here is "always." Far too often we've known people who thought the journey to serve God ended long before the end of their productive lives. Consider the priest or nun who says, "God called me to become a priest (or nun). Now that I am one, I have answered his call." Or consider the parent who says, "God called me to have a family. Now that I have one, I have answered my call." The same might go for schoolteachers, physicians, electricians, dance instructors, and business owners. However, most of the time when we take steps to answer our call, these steps along the way are not the ultimate answer to how we should live our lives, what we should ultimately contribute to the common good, or what we should do with our lives. These choices are merely milestones along the path toward ultimate fulfillment.

Every day you can ask yourself what you can do that particular day to ensure you are carrying out God's will in everything you do. Oftentimes the decision to become a mother or father, priest or nun, business owner or employee simply opens the door for thousands of additional decisions regarding one's call over an extended period of time. By seeking the best way to serve God's will in your current situation, you might find you need to change the circumstances.

For example, Martha had been a catechist for thirteen years when she was asked to become the director of religious education. This is a completely different role, requiring different skill sets and bringing a different set of responsibilities. Feeling called to fulfill this role, she accepted and enthusiastically set out to accomplish her goals. Many of the changes she implemented and the programs she started are still in existence, long after her departure. Later on, she was asked to chair the development committee to raise money for a new worship space. Feeling called to this role, she oversaw the raising of more than $8 million. What can we learn from this?

Each of these roles was different, and in each role she served God and others in very different ways. She learned a great deal from fulfilling each role. None of these represented what we might call her "ultimate" call, but collectively, they have each prepared her to make larger and more meaningful contributions to society through her service to God.

As long as we are confident that we are serving God at the present moment and remain open to different ways to serve him and human kind in the future, we can possess reasonable confidence that we are living our lives and answering our call in the best way possible.

Each decision we make about our circumstances and each choice we make about how we are going to answer our call brings us closer to God. Answering our call involves making all these choices, throughout our lives, to position ourselves to better serve God. Serving God is a culmination of life decisions and experiences—it is never a simple choice we make only once.

Hope

Through hope "we desire, and with steadfast trust await from God, eternal life and graces to merit it" (*CCC*, 1843). This virtue responds to the aspiration to happiness that God has placed in each of our hearts; it inspires and purifies our activities so that we may be prepared for the kingdom of heaven; it keeps us from discouragement; it sustains us during times of abandonment; it opens our hearts in expectation of eternal beatitude. Buoyed by hope we are preserved from selfishness and led to the happiness that flows from charity (*CCC*, 1818).

People often confuse hope with self-confidence or the optimism that things will turn out the way they want. People with true hope found their hope, not on themselves, but on God. An important way the virtue of hope comes into play when answering our call is that it helps us battle discouragement and despair when we suffer perceived setbacks. Instead, we should throw ourselves upon God with full confidence, trusting he will lead us where are meant to be.

We can think of no better example of this than a friend of ours who recently ran for elected political office. He said, "You know, I'm running for this seat at this time because a lot of people encouraged me to do so, and I think it's the right time and perhaps my mission in life at this time to serve our community at a different level. I believe I have the right skills and values to make a positive difference. I'm running the best campaign I can. But if the voters decide differently, I can't wait to see what God has in store for me next." Reflect for a moment on how different this is from the way many politicians think and act.

Many politicians define themselves and their worth in terms of whether they win or lose. They can't fathom the thought of losing and see this as a failure. Some even perceive it as an irreconcilable setback in their lives. Faithful people who possess hope react otherwise. They have confidence that if they maintain their belief in and commitment to God, he will, in turn, bestow his love on them and bring them to eternal happiness. This kind of certitude—not so much of the intellect, but coming from one's personal will and heart—is the kind of certitude that drives daggers into the soul of despair or desperation.

Hope does imply confidence, but it's a confidence in God and his love for us, rather than confidence in ourselves and what we accomplish in this world. Each of us can prove that we possess strong hope in spite of adversity, even when God seems to have abandoned us.

Charity

Through charity, "we love God above all things and our neighbors as ourselves for the love of God. Charity, the form of all the virtues, "binds everything together in perfect harmony" (*CCC*, 1844).

Faith causes us to adhere to God through knowledge. Accordingly, it is especially related to our intellect. Hope makes us adhere to God through the conviction that we will one day possess him in heaven. Accordingly, it is related to our desire for happiness. Charity seizes our entire being and by means of love, casts it into God. Accordingly, charity unites our affection to God in such a way that we no longer live for ourselves, but for God.[59]

Recently a friend of ours was being abused and persecuted by her supervisor at the hospital where she worked. Our friend had been hired while the supervisor was away on maternity leave. In her enthusiasm to do a good job, she took the initiative to solve several problems that had persisted for a while. The supervisor could have solved these problems but didn't. Upon returning, the supervisor heard numerous stories about how great this new employee was, how much initiative she had taken, and all the problems she had solved. Rather than greet the news with happiness, the supervisor became insecure and saw our friend as a threat to her job security and her role. The result was that the supervisor began to belittle our friend publicly and often and point out ridiculous minor discrepancies in her work.

After a time, however, another of our friend's coworkers took a bold and courageous action that demonstrated the essence of the charity-based love we aspire to with this virtue. She asked for a private meeting with the supervisor, where she shared with the supervisor her observations about what was happening. This coworker told the supervisor that she was bringing the issue to the supervisor's attention because other people were starting to comment and the supervisor's behavior was doing everyone, including the supervisor herself, a disservice. This is an example of "no one has greater love than this, to lay down his life for one's friends" (John 15:13, *NAB*), which is the ultimate act of Christian charity. The coworker was willing to risk her own security to aid a friend who was being abused and mistreated.

Integrating the Virtues Every Day

Your goal should be to live in accordance with all seven virtues every day of the week, letting the appropriate virtue guide your choices and your actions with every opportunity that presents itself. At the same time, consciously keeping all seven virtues at the forefront of your thought processes around the clock is virtually impossible. We have too much information to process already, without cycling through a checklist of seven virtues every time we have a choice to make or an action to take. So how do you go about making the virtues a more integral part of everything you do in the process of answering your call?

You integrate the virtues into your thought processes through the process of a daily critique. At the end of each day—perhaps during your evening prayer time or just before going to bed each night—you take time to reflect on one particular virtue. You ask yourself how many opportunities you had that day to make choices and take action that caused you to align yourself more closely with that particular virtue. Then you ask yourself what opportunities you see tomorrow or during the course of the next week to practice this particular virtue. It is a good idea to make a note of these anticipated opportunities so that when they arise you will have a reminder to think through your choices carefully and make better decisions than you might have made had you not thought it over in advance. During this inner conversation, try to recall instances where you applied the virtue correctly. When this happens, you can celebrate your success and pledge to replicate this behavior in the future.

We assign one of the seven virtues to each of seven days of the week, and we use the same virtue for the same day of the week each week. It is easier that way, and we found that, after a month or so, it became a habit for us. We no longer have to ask the question, "It's Monday; which virtue are we assessing today?" We now automatically know that Monday is the day we reflect on temperance. We've found that we gain more from this process if we do it together. Often one person's thinking triggers a thought in the other's mind, leading to deeper and more probing discussions. Frequently one of us will see something the other has missed.

No matter what process you use to make the virtues a more vital part of your life, you will find that this is a tangible and specific way to integrate God's grace with your gifts and purpose to achieve true fulfillment in answering your call.

CHAPTER TWENTY

Implement Your Plan

Remember to learn as you go. You change every day. The world around you changes every day. The people around you change every day. You must learn every day in order to ensure you are fulfilling your purpose in this new environment.

Lessons of Life

I feared being alone until I learned to like myself.

I feared failure until I realized that I only fail when I don't try.

I feared success until I realized that I had to try in order to be happy with myself.

I feared people's opinions until I learned that people would have opinions about me anyway.

I feared rejection until I learned to have faith in myself.

I feared pain until I learned that it's sometimes necessary for growth.

I feared the truth until I saw the ugliness in lies.

I feared life until I experienced its beauty.

I feared death until I realized that it's not an end, but a beginning.

I feared my destiny until I realized that I had the power to change my life.

I feared hate until I saw that it was nothing more than ignorance.

I feared love until it touched my heart, making the darkness
fade into endless sunny days.
I feared ridicule until I learned how to laugh at myself anew.
I feared growing old until I realized that I gained wisdom every
day.
I feared the future until I realized that life just kept getting
better.
I feared the past until I realized that it could no longer hurt me.
I feared the dark until I saw the beauty of the light.
I feared the light until I learned that the truth would give me
strength.
I feared change, until I saw that even the most beautiful
butterfly had to undergo a metamorphosis before it could fly.[60]

—Bobette Bryan

As Catholics we might add: "I feared many things until I learned the depth of Jesus's love for me and the power of the Holy Trinity and let them work in my life."

Daily Actions

As a Catholic, the following actions represent the *minimum* you should do to answer your call.

Start each day by offering that day to God. If you don't already have a daily morning prayer habit, consider praying like this each day when you awaken:

- Start with the Sign of the Cross.
- Say, "Glory be to the Father and to the Son, and to the Holy Spirit as it was in the beginning, is now, and shall be forever."
- Say, "Dear Lord, I offer this day to you. In addition, I offer my life and my career to you. Thank you for (name spouse). Thank

you for (name children and grandchildren). Thank you for (name other family members). Thank you for all the blessings, gifts, and opportunities you have given me. Please guide me. Help me to be a good spouse. Help me to be a good parent. Help me to stay faithful throughout the day. Please give me the wisdom, skills, energy, and resources to do magnificent work that brings glory and honor to you, serves the world, and touches people's lives in a special way."

Pray throughout the day. This can be accomplished in two ways. One way is by finding gifts of time throughout the day: pray a rosary during your morning commute; pray the Chaplet of Divine Mercy at three o'clock in the afternoon during your afternoon coffee break; take a short walk during lunch and pray a novena. Another way to pray throughout the day is by making your work and your actions throughout the day a prayer. Make a prayer of everything you do as a family member or worker in addition to the regular prayers you offer up. If you finish a task, complete it with magnificence as a way to honor God with your efforts.

Participate in the Eucharist regularly. Never miss Sunday Mass. Attend daily Mass whenever possible, and let divine graces flood into your heart.

Avoid busyness. Make good decisions about how you spend your time. If your activities contribute to your calling, you are spending your time and energy wisely. If they don't, you're not. One of the traps many people fall into is to say, "I didn't have enough time." When was the last time you made that statement? Was it yesterday? Last week? Whenever it was, how much time did you have? We all have the same amount of time: 24 hours in a day, 168 hours in a week, for 52 weeks each year. There's nothing you can do to get more or less time. You can't manage time, either—the term "time management" is a misnomer. The only thing you can manage is yourself in relation to time. You do that by making wise decisions about how you'll spend your time. The key is to choose to use the time you have available doing the things that are most important to you—even if they don't feel urgent. How do you decide what's important? You decide by first clarifying your life's purpose and then using your purpose as criteria for choosing how to spend the time you have available.

Avoid sin. Sin puts distance between you and God. The greater the separation from God, the more difficult it will be to live your calling. Avoiding sin also means regular participation in the sacrament of reconciliation.

Be optimistic. The Salesian faith tradition founded by St. Francis de Sales extols joyful optimism as one of its virtues. Indeed, being optimistic is part of being Christian—not some kind of naïve, Pollyanna optimism that pretends things are better than they are, but a rock-solid trust in God's intervention to save us and work on our behalf. Without optimism we can't possibly do what God requires of us.

Periodically pray "The Novena to Answer Your Call" (see end of chapter), either by yourself or with your spouse. In biblical times the number nine symbolized "perfection times perfection." Novena is derived from the Latin word *novem,* which means nine. It was also thought that symbolically, nine days represented the perfect amount of time to pray. It was customary for the ancient Greeks and Romans to mourn for nine days after a death. Early Christians offered Mass for a deceased person for nine days. Novenas to certain saints became popular during the Middle Ages.[61]

Celebrating Mass and participating in the sacraments are the highest form of prayer. But devotions such as novenas also have a special place in Catholic life. The dinner feast may be a culmination, the time you are fed the most, but breakfast gets your day started right. Novenas offered to specific saints can help us witness more strongly to our faith and to copy their examples of holiness and service.[62]

Regularly refocus your commitment and transform your energy into action. Remember the teachings of St. Francis de Sales, who said that the ultimate test of prayer is a person's actions: "To be an angel in prayer and a beast in one's relations with people is to go lame on both legs."

> Deep within his conscience man discovers a law which he has not laid upon himself but which he must obey. Its voice, ever calling him to love and to do good and to avoid evil, sounds in his heart at the right moment....
>
> —*CCC*, 1776

The Novena to Answer Your Call

The Novena to Answer Your Call is a nine-day devotion offered through St. Michael, St. Thomas Aquinas, and St. Joseph. You can pray it by yourself, but we encourage you to pray it together with your spouse (substituting "we" for "I" throughout, etc.). The novena uses the nine dimensions of call for its framework, focusing for three days on bringing God's supernatural grace into every dimension of our lives (through the intercession of St. Michael), three days on nurturing our natural gifts (through the intercession of St. Thomas Aquinas), and three days on fulfilling our unique life's purpose (through the intercession of St. Joseph). Although all three saints are the focus of devotion for all nine days, special prayers are offered to St. Michael during the first three days, to St. Thomas Aquinas during the second three days, and to St. Joseph during the final three days.

St. Michael the Archangel's feast day is September 29. The name Michael signifies "Who is like to God?" It was the war cry of the good angels in the battle fought in heaven against Satan and his followers. Holy Scripture describes St. Michael as "one of the chief princes" and leader of the forces of heaven. We turn to him to help protect God's supernatural grace at work in our life and to keep us close to God at all times.

St. Thomas Aquinas is priest and doctor of the Church and patron of all universities and students. His feast day is January 28. He was a great student and a man of great virtue; he studied under St. Albert the Great and became a great teacher and writer. St. Thomas was one of the greatest and most influential theologians of all time. He was canonized in 1323 and declared a doctor of the Church by Pope Pius V. We turn to him for assistance in developing our natural gifts and to ask his help and guidance in using those gifts in such a way that we bring glory and honor to God.

St. Joseph is foster father of Jesus, carpenter, spouse, head of the Holy Family, and a righteous man before God. His feast day is March 19. We turn to him as a perfect example of the nine dimensions of our call fulfilled.

First Day

Pray: Glory be to the Father and to the Son and to the Holy Spirit, as it was in the beginning and shall be forever. Amen.

Pray: I humbly call upon St. Michael, St. Thomas Aquinas, and St. Joseph to intercede on my behalf before the throne of God. I beg that you obtain for me the blessings necessary to completely answer my call. I ask to be filled with spiritual and physical energy that will allow me to fully know, love, and serve God in this life in order to share eternal happiness with him in the next. Please ask him to grant the petitions I seek which include filling my heart with faith, fully developing my natural gifts, and carrying out the unique purpose he has given me.

On this first day of the novena I humbly ask St. Michael the Archangel to come especially close. Protect me and my family from everything evil and guide me to God's graces so that I may in rely on God's supernatural grace to answer my call.

Our Father…

Hail Mary…

Pray: St. Michael the Archangel, defend us in battle. Be our defense against the wickedness and snares of the devil. May God rebuke him, we humbly pray. And you, O Prince of the heavenly host, banish into hell Satan and the other evil spirits who roam through the world seeking the ruin of souls. Amen.

Second Day

Pray: Glory be to the Father and to the Son and to the Holy Spirit as it was in the beginning and shall be forever. Amen.

Pray: I humbly call upon St. Michael, St. Thomas Aquinas, and St. Joseph to intercede on my behalf before the throne of God. I beg that you obtain for me the blessings necessary to completely answer my call. I ask to be filled with spiritual and physical energy that will allow me to fully know, love, and serve God in this life in order to share eternal happiness with him in the next. Please ask him to grant the petitions I seek, which include filling my heart with faith, fully developing my natural gifts, and carrying out the unique purpose he has given me.

On this second day of the novena, I humbly ask St. Michael the Archangel, as one of the chief princes of heaven and as a leader of the forces of heaven, to lead me closer to the sacraments and help to clarify for me a path here on earth that will lead me to heaven where I can join you in the presence of the Lord, surrounded by all that is good. Help me to become a holy warrior like you defending the faith and honoring God in all I do.

Our Father...

Hail Mary...

Pray: Glorious St. Michael, Prince of the heavenly hosts, valiant defender of the Church, you are always ready to assist the people of God in times of adversity. Be with me whenever I face difficulty that I may walk steadfastly along the way of discipleship. I have confidence that through your intercession the Lord will grant me all the spiritual graces and strength that I need to follow Jesus more closely, and that one day I may rejoice forever with you in heaven. Amen.

Third Day

Pray: Glory be to the Father and to the Son and to the Holy Spirit as it was in the beginning and shall be forever.

Pray: I humbly call upon St. Michael, St. Thomas Aquinas, and St. Joseph to intercede on my behalf before the throne of God. I beg that you obtain for me the blessings necessary to completely answer my call. I ask to be filled with spiritual and physical energy that will allow me to fully know, love, and serve God in this life in order to share eternal happiness with him in the next. Please ask him to grant the petitions I seek, which include filling my heart with faith, fully developing my natural gifts, and carrying out the unique purpose he has given me.

On this third day of the novena, I humbly ask St. Michael the Archangel to remind me always that prayer without action is not enough. Just as you stood up against the evil forces attacking heaven, each of us must follow your example to confront the evil that surrounds us and pollutes the world in which we live. Share with me your courage. Share with me your faith. Share with me your full devotion to God so that I may someday join you in heaven. Help me to become a holy warrior like you, defending the faith and honoring God in all I do.

Our Father...

Hail Mary...

Pray: O God, you made blessed Michael the Archangel victorious in the battle against evil. I ask that, with the cross of your Son as my banner, I, too, may be victorious in the spiritual conflicts I face in my daily life. Through the intercession of St. Michael, deliver me from all evil and keep temptation far from me. Guide me to faithfully follow your will and to walk in the way of your commandments. I ask this through Christ, our Lord. Amen.

Fourth Day

Pray: Glory be to the Father and to the Son and to the Holy Spirit as it was in the beginning and shall be forever.

Pray: I humbly call upon St. Michael, St. Thomas Aquinas, and St. Joseph to intercede on my behalf before the throne of God. I beg that you obtain for me the blessings necessary to completely answer my call. I ask to be filled with spiritual and physical energy that will allow me to fully know, love, and serve God in this life in order to share eternal happiness with him in the next. Please ask him to grant the petitions I seek, which include filling my heart with faith, fully developing my natural gifts, and carrying out the unique purpose he has given me.

On this fourth day of the novena, I humbly ask St. Thomas Aquinas, outstanding student and scholar, to help me develop my natural gifts and talents so they can be used to their fullest to bring glory and honor to God. Help me to discover new gifts and to realize the potential of gifts that I have not used to the fullest potential thus far. Help me to reflect honestly and free from pride regarding my gifts so they can be used according to God's will.

Our Father...

Hail Mary...

Pray: St. Thomas Aquinas, I ask that you watch over me and intervene on my behalf as I humbly ask God, the true fount of wisdom and the noble origin of all things, to be pleased to shed light on the darkness of mind in which I was born, the twofold beam of his light and warmth to dispel my ignorance and sin. I also ask that he instruct my speech and touch my lips with graciousness. Make me keen to understand, quick to learn, and able to remember. Make me delicate to interpret and ready to speak.

I also humbly ask that he please also guide me in all my endeavors going forward. Amen.

Fifth Day

Pray: Glory be to the Father and to the Son and to the Holy Spirit as it was in the beginning and shall be forever.

Pray: I humbly call upon St. Michael, St. Thomas Aquinas, and St. Joseph to intercede on my behalf before the throne of God. I beg that you obtain for me the blessings necessary to completely answer my call. I ask to be filled with spiritual and physical energy that will allow me to fully know, love, and serve God in this life in order to share eternal happiness with him in the next. Please ask him to grant the petitions I seek, which include filling my heart with faith, fully developing my natural gifts, and carrying out the unique purpose he has given me.

On this fifth day of the novena, I humbly ask St. Thomas Aquinas to help me discover new gifts and talents and the potential to develop gifts and talents that I have not yet developed. Throughout history many great people have discovered talents and gifts late in life that were used to serve you and the world in a special way. Please help me to identify any such gifts I possess so that I may honor God through their development and application. Never let me lose sight of the fact that any such talents are truly gifts from God and therefore should be used in his service.

Our Father…

Hail Mary…

Pray: In the words of St. Thomas Aquinas, I humbly ask that you grant me, O Lord our God, a mind to know you, a heart to seek you, wisdom to find you, conduct pleasing to you, faithful perseverance in waiting for you, and a hope of finally embracing you. Amen.

Sixth Day

Pray: Glory be to the Father and to the Son and to the Holy Spirit as it was in the beginning and shall be forever.

Pray: I humbly call upon St. Michael, St. Thomas Aquinas, and St. Joseph to intercede on my behalf before the throne of God. I beg that you obtain for me the blessings necessary to completely answer my call. I ask to be filled with spiritual and physical energy that will allow me to fully know, love, and serve God in this life in order to share eternal happiness with him in the next. Please ask him to grant the petitions I seek, which include filling my heart with faith, fully developing my natural gifts, and carrying out the unique purpose he has given me.

On this sixth day of the novena, I humbly ask St. Thomas Aquinas for guidance to help me to fully develop those gifts that are collaborative or cooperative in nature, meaning gifts such as teamwork, developing positive interpersonal relationships, and working in support of the efforts of others. Guide me so that I may always bring out the best in others and help to develop their gifts to their fullest potential. Let my cooperative example become contagious so that everyone I work with will want to follow the teachings of our Savior, Jesus Christ.

Our Father…

Hail Mary…

Pray: O God, who has enlightened Your Church with the wonderful learning of blessed Thomas Aquinas, your confessor, and renders it fruitful by his holy works, grant me, I beseech thee, both to understand that which he taught and to follow his example in what he practiced. Through our Lord Jesus Christ, Thy Son, Who lives and reigns with the Holy Ghost, One God, world without end. Amen.

Seventh Day

Pray: Glory be to the Father and to the Son and to the Holy Spirit as it was in the beginning and shall be forever.

Pray: I humbly call upon St. Michael, St. Thomas Aquinas, and St. Joseph to intercede on my behalf before the throne of God. I beg that you obtain for me the blessings necessary to completely answer my call. I ask to be filled with spiritual and physical energy that will allow me to fully know, love, and serve God in this life in order to share eternal happiness with him in the next. Please ask him to grant the petitions I seek, which include filling my heart with faith, fully developing my natural gifts, and carrying out the unique purpose he has given me.

On this seventh day of the novena, I humbly ask St. Joseph, as a family man in the roles of spouse and foster father of our Lord, to help me in my role as spouse, parent, and child to follow your righteous example. Help me to nurture all members of my family so that I may provide for their spiritual, psychological, and intellectual development while helping to provide for their safety and physical needs.

Our Father…

Hail Mary…

Pray: Heavenly Father, I thank you for the gift of my family and for the many joys and blessings that have come to me through each of them. Help me to appreciate the uniqueness of each while celebrating the diversity of all. Through the intercession of St. Joseph, foster father of your Son, I ask you to protect my family from the evils of this world. Grant me all the power to forgive when I have been hurt and the humility to ask for forgiveness when I have caused pain. Unite me in the love of your Son, Jesus, so that I may be a sign of the unity you desire for all humanity. Amen.

Eighth Day

Pray: Glory be to the Father and to the Son and to the Holy Spirit as it was in the beginning and shall be forever.

Pray: I humbly call upon St. Michael, St. Thomas Aquinas, and St. Joseph to intercede on my behalf before the throne of God. I beg that you obtain for me the blessings necessary to completely answer my call. I ask to be filled with spiritual and physical energy that will allow me to fully know, love, and serve God in this life in order to share eternal happiness with him in the next. Please ask him to grant the petitions I seek, which include filling my heart with faith, fully developing my natural gifts, and carrying out the unique purpose he has given me.

On this eighth day of the novena, I humbly ask St. Joseph to help me to be a living example of the Word of God in everything I do. Help me to cheerfully and lovingly carry out all my work-related activities in a way that brings glory and honor to God and brings my soul ever into deeper union with him. Help me to disdain mediocrity and strive to be magnificent in all I do.

Our Father…

Hail Mary…

Pray: St. Joseph, example for all those who work to support themselves and their families, obtain for me the grace to labor with thankfulness and joy. Grant that I may consider my daily endeavors as opportunities to use and develop the gifts of nature and grace I have received from God. In the workplace may I mirror your virtues of integrity, moderation, patience, and inner peace, treating my coworkers with kindness and respect. May all I do and say lead others to the Lord and bring honor to God's name. Amen.

Ninth Day

Pray: Glory be to the Father and to the Son and to the Holy Spirit as it was in the beginning and shall be forever.

Pray: I humbly call upon St. Michael, St. Thomas Aquinas, and St. Joseph to intercede on my behalf before the throne of God. I beg that you obtain for me the blessings necessary to completely answer my call. I ask to be filled with spiritual and physical energy that will allow me to fully know, love, and serve God in this life in order to share eternal happiness with him in the next. Please ask him to grant the petitions I seek, which include filling my heart with faith, fully developing my natural gifts, and carrying out the unique purpose he has given me.

On this ninth day of the novena, I humbly ask St. Joseph to guide me through my life here on earth. Just as you listened to the Spirit's inspiration to flee to Egypt even though it meant hardship and struggle, help me listen to God at work in my life. Just as you were a caring parent and devoted spouse, able to protect and provide for Jesus and Mary in an unfamiliar and hostile land, let me provide likewise for my family. Please obtain for me the grace to always listen to the voice of conscience urging me to fulfill my promise so I can earn eternal happiness.

Our Father...

Hail Mary...

Pray: Oh glorious St. Joseph, steadfast follower of Jesus Christ, I am confident that your prayers for me will be heard at the throne of God. To you I lift up my heart and hands asking your powerful intercession to obtain from the compassionate heart of Jesus all the graces necessary for my spiritual and temporal well-being, particularly the grace of a happy death, and the special grace for which this novena is offered, which is to answer my call here on earth. St. Joseph, guardian of the Word incarnate, by the love you bear for Jesus Christ, and for the glory of his name, hear my prayer and obtain my petitions. Amen.

1. Edward Flood, Tr., *Stronger Than Hatred* (Hyde Park, N.Y.: New City, 1988).

2. *Meditations and Devotions of the Late Cardinal Newman* (New York: Longman, Green, 1911), p. 301.

3. Quoted at http://thinkexist.com/quotation/consult_not_your_fears_but_your_hopes_and_your/8220.html.

4. "Oprah Talks to Bill Clinton," *O, The Oprah Magazine,* August 2004.

5. Josemaría Escriva, *The Way: The Essential Classic of Opus Dei's Founder* (New York: Image, 1982), 817, 813, 814, 815.

6. Available at http://articles.cnn.com/2001-09-14/us/Falwell.apology_1_thomas-road-baptist-church-jerry-falwell-feminists?_s=PM:US.

7. *USA Today,* October 4, 2001.

8. Dr. Andrew Newberg and Eugene d'Aquili, *Why God Won't Go Away: Brain Science and the Biology of Belief* (New York: Ballantine, 2001).

9. Dr. James Austin, *Zen and the Brain* (Cambridge, Mass.: MIT Press, 1998).

10. Helen E. Buckley, originally published in *School Arts Magazine* in October 1961.

11. *Tobias* magazine, Fall 2010, p. 64.

12. Twitter, @CardinalDolan, July 30, 2012.

13. Escriva, Josemaria. *The Way.* Sceptor, S.A. 1982, #267.

14. Mary Mark Wickenhiser, FSP, *St. Joseph Novena and Prayers* (Boston: Pauline, 2004), p. 35.

15. Wickenhiser, pp. 35–36.

16. Address of John Paul II to the bishops attending a formation course sponsored by the Congregation for Bishops, Thursday, September 18, 2003.

17. *CCC,* 1999–2003.

18. *CCC,* 1999–2003.

19. *CCC,* 1999–2003.

20. *CCC,* 1999–2003.

21. *Baltimore Catechism,* #3, from the Third Plenary Council of Baltimore, 1891 version, Q.150. (Available at http://www.baltimore-catechism.com/index.htm).

22. *Baltimore Catechism,* #3.

23. *The Confessions of St. Augustine,* a new translation by Rex Warner (New York: New American Library, 1963), p. 235.

24. Jennifer Fulwiler, "5 Questions Before You Leave the Catholic Church," *National Catholic Register,* May 30, 2012.

25. St. Nilus Sorsky, 1433–1508, from *A Treasury of Russian Spirituality,* G.P. Fedotov, 1965.

26. William Barclay, *The Plain Man's Book of Prayers* (n.p.: Fount, 1997).

27. Benedict XVI, Encyclical Letter *Deus Caritas Est,* 14.

28. Mitch Albom interview, CatholicMatch.com, November 21, 2011. Available at http://www.catholicmatch.com/blog/2011/11/mitch-albom-faith-begins-with-%E2%80%98the-smallest-act%E2%80%99-video/.

29. Benedict XVI, Encyclical Letter *Deus Caritas Est,* 18.

30. Address by Most Rev. Charles J. Chaput, O.F.M., Cap, "The Priestly Vocation, 2005: Co-authoring the Future with God," December 6, 2005, Philadelphia. Available at http://www.archden.org/archbishop_writings_discourses/addresses/addresses_Dec06_05_PriestlyVocation.pdf.

31. Chaput, emphasis added.

32. Chaput. Note: The material in this chapter draws heavily from this address given by Archbishop Chaput in 2005. We consider his many writings and teachings unparalleled. For years he has given us a foundation for understanding our faith and how to live our faith

that is indispensable. His comments during that address couldn't have been better stated, and the theme overlaps significantly with the theme of this chapter. However, his remarks addressed priests, and our audience for this book is all people. We've relied heavily on his ideas. Our adaptations have been to expand them for our broader audience. This has made it difficult to discern where to properly add footnotes. Rather than have a chapter with a dozens of footnotes, we've chosen to use just this one to give full credit to Archbishop Chaput.

33. http://www.catholicnewsagency.com/document.php?n=207

34. Quoting Gaudium et Spes, 37, section 2.

35. Chaput, emphasis added.

36. Bl. John Paul II quoted in Chaput.

37. Pope John Paul II, Message of the Holy Father to Youth Meeting in Santiago de Compostela, August 8, 1999. Available at http://www.vatican.va/holy_father/john_paul_ii/speeches/1999/august/documents/hf_jp-ii_mes_08081999_youth-compostela_en.html.

38. *Collected Works of Saint John of the Cross,* translated by Kieran Kavanaugh and Otilio Rodriguez (Washington, D.C.: ICS, 1991). The Dark Night, book 2: chapters 13:11; 16:4,7 Strength in Darkness: Wisdom from John of the Cross, O'Reilly Media, 2011, p. xx.

39. St. Thomas Aquinas, *Exposition on John,* chapter 14, lecture 2. Quoted at http://www.crossroadsinitiative.com/pics/Thomas_Way.pdf.

40. "The Father Factor—Crime on the Increase in Dad-Free Zones," Tim Drake, *The National Catholic Register*, December 17–23, 2006, page 7.

41. Drake, p. 1. Available at http://www.ncregister.com/site/article/1604.

42. Drake, p. 7.

43. Drake, p. 7.

44. Drake, p. 7.

45. Drake, p. 7.

46. "The Teenager and the Porn Star," *LA Magazine,* November, 2006, pp. 152–274.

47. Address of John Paul II to the Plenary Assembly of the Pontifical Council for the Family, Friday, October 18, 2002, paragraphs 2 and 3, referencing *Dies Domini,* 81, *Letter to Families,* 10, and *CCC,* 1608.

48. Citing *Familiaris Consortio,* 21; cf. *Lumen Gentium,* 11; cf. Ephesians 5:21—6:4; Colossians 3:18–21; 1 Peter 3:1–7.

49. Referencing *Gravissimum Educationis,* 52, section 1.

50. Citing Sirach 7:27–28.

51. Citing *Gravissimum Educationis,* 3, cf. *Familiaris Consortio,* 36.

52. Phil Rivers quote from Sept/Oct 2012 issue of *Family Foundations,* published by the Couple to Couple League.

53. Gregory F.A. Pierce, *Spirituality at Work: 10 Ways to Balance Your Life on the Job* (Chicago: Loyola, 2001), pp. 17–18.

54. Cf. *Gaudium et Spes,* 64.

55. Cf. Genesis 1:28, 34; *Centisimus Annus,* 31; 2 Thessalonians 3:10; cf. 1 Thessalonians 4:11; cf. Genesis 3:14-19; cf. *Laborem Exercens,* 27.

56. *The Catholic Business Hour,* August 11, 2012.

57. *CCC,* 1803–1845.

58. *The Catholic Business Hour with Dick Lyles,* broadcast Saturday mornings on EWTN's global Catholic radio network.

59. Rev. Fr. Gabriel of St. Mary Magdalen O.C.D., *Divine Intimacy* (Rockford, Ill.: Tan, 1996), p. 747.

60. Quoted at uncomfortablesoul.com/page/4. Bryan's site is http://www.cookiecreation.com/index.html.

61. Mary Mark, Wickenhiser, FSP, *Saint Michael, Novenas and Prayers* (Boston: Pauline, 2004), pp. 4–7.

62. Wickenhiser, pp. 35–36.